T0028294

MY UTMOST FOR HIS HIGHEST®

MODERN CLASSIC EDITION

A 90-Day Gift Devotional

MY UTMOST FOR HIS HIGHEST®

MODERN CLASSIC EDITION

OSWALD CHAMBERS

Adapted by Macy Halford

Our Daily Bread
Publishing™

Authorized by the Oswald Chambers Publications Association Ltd.

My Utmost for His Highest®: A 90-Day Gift Devotional, Modern Classic Edition
© 2023 by Oswald Chambers Publications Association Ltd.

With your purchase of this Authorized edition, both the Oswald Chambers Publications Association Ltd. and Our Daily Bread Ministries are able to provide resources and assistance to their respective global networks, partners, and individuals.

Interior design by Michael J. Williams

ISBN: 978-1-64070-214-1

Library of Congress Cataloging-in-Publication Data Available

Printed in China
23 24 25 26 27 28 29 30 / 8 7 6 5 4 3 2 1

CONTENTS

PREFACE

Has there ever been a book quite like *My Utmost for His Highest*? Since it first appeared in England in 1927, the so-called *golden book* of Oswald Chambers has traversed languages and countries and denominations to become one of the best-selling daily devotionals of all time. Published ten years after the death of its author, a Scottish preacher who lived and died in relative obscurity, it has established itself as a living document, playing a vital role in the daily spiritual experience of millions. It is a classic, to be sure, but one which lives on the reader's bedside table rather than the collector's shelf.

I received my first copy of *My Utmost for His Highest* when I was fifteen, but I was aware of it long before then. It is a book that sat on my grandmother's bedside table, and on my mother's; a book that was spoken of often during the coffee hour following Sunday service or at the Wednesday evening Bible study. In the place and time where I grew up—Dallas, Texas, in the 1980s and '90s—Chambers was so well known and so well loved that people referred to him simply as "Oswald," and for them that name had become synonymous with his most famous book. "Have you read Oswald today?" people would ask.

The conversations that would follow were so lively and immediate that I remember being shocked when I first learned the basic details of Oswald's biography. He wasn't, as I'd supposed, a pastor one might hear on the radio; you wouldn't find him on a speaking tour of local libraries. He was a painter-turned-preacher of no specific denomination who'd been born in 1874 and who'd died during the First World War.

Yet it didn't take me long, after I began reading *Utmost*, to understand Oswald's appeal. My grandmother had warned me that I might find him challenging at first, but had urged me to give him a chance. (Her exact words, if I recall correctly, were "Oswald ain't easy, but he's worth it.") The challenging part was true enough. *Utmost* was full of ideas drawn from theology, philosophy, and psychology; its language was sophisticated and fairly dated. In many places, though, it was entirely accessible. Each entry contained some gem—some profound reading of Scripture, some meditation on the Holy Spirit, some astute advice on living the life of a Christian disciple—that made *Utmost* seem as though it had just been written, and just for me.

If there is a single quality shared by all classic works of literature, it must be *timelessness*—a word which surely describes *My Utmost for His Highest*. It is a forever book, a book that will always belong to *right now*. Why, then, a new version? Does it even make sense to speak of "updating" a book that belongs to forever?

The answer to that is rooted in the story of *Utmost*'s creation, a story for a long time unknown to the general public. This began to change in 1993, with the publication of the first full-length biography of Chambers, David McCasland's *Abandoned to God*. Since then, numerous projects have delved into the history of Chambers's work (including my own contribution, *My Utmost: A Devotional Memoir*, published in 2017), bringing the story of *Utmost* to a wider audience.

Summarized briefly, the story of *Utmost* is the story of a Scottish preacher, Oswald Chambers, who fell in love with an English stenographer, Gertrude Hobbs, in 1908 on a boat bound for America. He was going over to preach, she to look for secretarial work. Almost immediately, the two discovered that they shared numerous passions: a passionate interest in Jesus Christ, a passionate interest in Christian discipleship, and a passionate interest in the written word. On this journey, Oswald gave Gertrude the name she would go by for the rest of her life—Biddy, from B.D., for "Beloved Disciple"—and the two dreamed up their future publishing endeavor. In one of his earliest letters to Biddy, Oswald wrote:

It will be such a meagre home we will have, you and myself going heart and soul into literary and itinerating work for Him. It will be hard and glorious and arduous. I want us to write and preach; if I could talk to you and you shorthand it down and then type it, what ground we could get over! I wonder if it kindles you as it does me!

Oswald and Biddy wed in England in 1910, after which they took jobs at a Bible training college on the outskirts of London. Oswald gave lectures and sermons; Biddy took notes. In 1913, their daughter, Kathleen, was born, and in 1915, following the outbreak of the war, the family decamped to the Egyptian desert, where Oswald was to serve as chaplain to British troops. In the desert, Oswald continued giving talks, and Biddy continued writing them down. When he died, in an army field hospital in 1917, following surgery for appendicitis, Biddy had amassed enough notes to fill more than fifty books. This is precisely what she went on to do, dedicating the remaining forty-nine years of her life to bringing Oswald's teaching to the world.

In this undertaking, Biddy was aided by a small, rotating group of friends and Oswald Chambers devotees—volunteers who came together to help oversee the printing and distribution of his work. Formally incorporated in 1942 as the Oswald Chambers Publications Association, the group had (and continues to have) a particular mission: to keep Oswald's work in circulation, pouring any proceeds back into the support of charitable causes and future editions. Thanks in part to this arrangement, Biddy had enormous freedom in dealing with Oswald's words. Every editorial choice was hers, and every choice was made not for the demands of the market but—as she herself would have put it—for the glory of God.

Over the past decades, as the body of Chambers scholarship has grown, the impact of Biddy's editorial choices has become clear. Biddy's aim wasn't so much to produce books *based on* Oswald's talks; it was to reproduce the talks themselves, word for word. This approach has many advantages, chief among them a sense of intimacy and immediacy;

reading Oswald now, one still hears his voice ringing through. But it also has its drawbacks. Oswald was a wonderful speaker, but he never used notes or outlines. He spoke as the Spirit moved him, peppering his talks with quotations drawn from that most unreliable of sources—human memory. He also tended to talk at length, introducing a topic and exploring it in depth. Most printed versions of his talks are many thousands of words long.

The most notable exception is, of course, *My Utmost for His Highest.* Composed entirely of excerpts, *Utmost* was itself a kind of shorthand. By design, each of its entries was taken out of context. By design, each entry left out any information Oswald himself didn't include. Any quotation or bit of Scripture Oswald failed to attribute remained unattributed; any mistaken reference remained mistaken. Biddy was ever faithful to Oswald's spoken word.

Clearly, Biddy's hands-off approach to *Utmost* didn't hurt the book's prospects. Yet it bears mentioning that a very different approach was taken to the few works which were published during Oswald's lifetime—that is, to the articles and pamphlets he himself prepared for publication. In the writings collected in the two-volume *Christian Disciplines,* for instance, the numerous quotations are accurately reproduced and attributed; repetitions are few and far between; the message is sculpted; and the context of any given point is clear. When the current members of the Oswald Chambers Publications Association first approached me with the idea of updating *Utmost,* what immediately sprang into my mind was *Christian Disciplines*—a work with a level of polish that allows Oswald's message to shine.

My goal, then, for this Modern Classic Edition of *My Utmost for His Highest* has been to bring clarity and readability, while preserving Chambers's message and voice. In several instances, I've gone back to the original sermons and lectures from which the excerpts were taken in an effort to grasp their wider context. The vocabulary has been updated, though many choice "Oswaldisms" remain (see the glossary that follows). For biblical references, the New International Version has replaced the King

James Version, except where Oswald's original depends on a word or phrase found only in the KJV.

Throughout, my aim has been not only to honor Oswald's intentions for the messages in *Utmost*, but also Biddy's. It seems fitting to give the final word to her—the woman responsible for bringing Oswald Chambers's words to the world. "It is because," Biddy Chambers wrote in her foreword to the first edition, October 1927,

> it is felt that the author is one to whose teaching men will return, that this book has been prepared, and it is sent out with the prayer that day by day the messages may continue to bring the quickening life and inspiration of the Holy Spirit.

May they continue to do so.

Macy Halford
Strasbourg, France
July 2022

UNDERSTANDING OSWALD CHAMBERS'S
LANGUAGE AND THEOLOGY

A GLOSSARY OF TERMS

Abandon, abandonment (to God). To fully give oneself over to God. In Chambers's usage, "abandon" and "abandonment" carry no negative connotation (in the sense of *being* abandoned or lost). Rather, "abandoning oneself to God" is an active, positive choice, freely undertaken by those who wish to commit themselves to the Lord.

Amateur providence. Generally used to describe a spiritual leader who is trying to place him- or herself at the center of another person's spiritual experience—right where Jesus Christ should be.

Baptism of the Holy Spirit. Chambers defines this baptism, which is distinct from baptism by water, as "an invasion" by the Holy Spirit. He bases his understanding on the description of Pentecost (Acts 2:1–13) and on Jesus's declaration in Acts 1:8: "You will receive power when the Holy Spirit comes on you." To receive the baptism of the Holy Spirit, in Chambers's view, one must ask: "How much more will your Father in heaven give the Holy Spirit to those who ask him!" (Luke 11:13).

Born from above. Another term for the baptism of the Holy Spirit, the baptism that makes sanctification possible (see "sanctification"). It is distinct from both salvation and baptism by water.

Broken bread and poured-out wine. From the account of the Last Supper in Luke 22, Chambers uses it to describe how the Christian disciple should allow him- or herself to be used in Christ's hands. Despite carrying the ritualistic overtones of the Eucharist, this phrase isn't employed in that sense by Chambers, who belonged to no specific denomination or theological tradition.

Disciple. A Christian who has answered a divine call to devote his or her life to following Christ and preaching the gospel. For Chambers, not every Christian receives the call to discipleship.

Educate (down) to the scruple. Chambers uses it to mean that God inspects and brings to light every single aspect of our lives and personalities, no matter how small.

Intercession / Intervention. Chambers uses these two words interchangeably to indicate a specific kind of prayer: going to God on behalf of other people, in order to learn his will for them. For Chambers, "intercessory prayer" is distinct from self-centered—and wrongful—prayer, in which we go to God seeking blessings for ourselves.

Saint. Chambers uses this word to signify a Christian who has undergone the baptism of the Holy Spirit and has been sanctified (see "sanctification"), whose thinking and behavior clearly reflect this spiritual rebirth.

Salvation. For Chambers, this is the "first sovereign work of grace," accomplished for us by Jesus Christ on the cross. It is distinct from sanctification, the "second mighty work of grace" (see "sanctification"). All Christians, for Chambers, have undergone the experience of salvation, but not all have been sanctified.

Sanctification / Entire Sanctification. A cornerstone of Chambers's theology, based primarily on 1 Thessalonians 4: "It is God's will that you should be sanctified." Chambers's elaboration of the concept draws on the Holiness theology of John Wesley, one of Chambers's favorite thinkers. For Wesley, the baptism of the Holy Spirit was a second work of grace, following and distinct from salvation. In imparting the Holy

Spirit, sanctification also imparted the ability to lead a sinless, "perfect" life. The doctrine has always been the subject of intense theological debate. Chambers embraced the idea of sanctification (see "baptism of the Holy Spirit") but refused to get entangled in the perfectionism debate. For Chambers, sanctification wasn't simply a single spiritual baptism; it was a way of living: "Sanctification is not *once for all, but once for always*. Sanctification is an instantaneous, continuous work of grace. . . . Sanctification means we have the glorious opportunity of proving daily, hourly, momentarily, this identity with Jesus Christ" (from *The Moral Foundations of Life*).

Vision. Chambers uses the word "vision" to denote several different types of spiritual insight, all of them meaning, in essence, an idea of some future occurrence which God brings to a person's mind. The vision might be of a future event; a purpose God wishes the person to fulfill; or something more vague, like a future state of being. Often, Chambers declined to specify what type of vision he was talking about, leaving the interpretation up to the reader.

MY UTMOST FOR HIS HIGHEST®

MODERN CLASSIC EDITION

90 READINGS

Let Us Keep to the Point

I eagerly expect and hope that I will in no way be ashamed,
but will have sufficient courage so that now as always Christ
will be exalted in my body, whether by life or by death.

PHILIPPIANS 1:20

My utmost for his highest. To be all for God; to act with boldness, expressing Christ in every word and deed. This, Paul says, is how to walk through life unashamed.

The journey isn't a journey of reason or debate. We can't think or argue our way through it. It is a journey of surrender, of abandoning ourselves to God, absolutely and forever.

There will always be good reasons not to. We debate with God, telling him that we are concerned for others, that if we start on the journey, our loved ones will suffer. Really, we are worried for ourselves, for our own comfort and safety. We tell God he doesn't know what he's asking.

Keep to the point: he *does* know. Shut out your worries and stand before God with one thing only in your heart: *my utmost for his highest.* Determine to be absolutely and entirely for him and him alone.

My best for his glory. At first, the call comes gently. Then it grows louder, until finally God produces a crisis in our lives that demands we make a choice. For or against; yes or no; stay or go.

Has the crisis come to you? If it has, *go.* Paul, like Christ, would let nothing deter him, whether it meant life or death. As a new year dawns, let us embrace this same spirit, surrendering all with boldness and with joy.

The Unplanned Journey

By faith Abraham . . . obeyed and went,
even though he did not know where he was going.

HEBREWS 11:8

Have you ever set off on an unplanned journey, taking, as Christ instructed, no thought for your life, no thought for what you would eat or drink or wear (Matthew 6:25)?

"Where are you going, and what will you do?" If you begin to live for God, people will ask you this all the time. But if you are living in the way Christ wants, you won't have a logical answer: there is none. You can't know what you're going to do; you can't know what God is going to do. All you can know is that God knows. This is what it means to trust entirely in him.

Have you been begging God to tell you his plans? He never will. God doesn't tell us what he's going to do; he *reveals* to us *who he is*. It is through taking action, through stepping out in faith, that we receive this revelation. Ask yourself: Do I believe in a miracle-working God, and will I step out in surrender to him until I am not surprised one iota at anything he does? To step out in this way is to journey beyond your convictions and creeds and past experiences, until, as far as your faith is concerned, there is nothing at all between yourself and God.

Imagine, for a moment, that God really is who he says he is: the God of your days and your nights, of your future and your past; the God of all. What an impertinence worry is! Set aside your worries, and let your attitude be one of eager adventure.

The Grace of God's Forgetting

For it is by grace you have been saved, through faith—
and this is not from yourselves, it is the gift of God.

EPHESIANS 2:8

No one can be saved by their own efforts. We have the sneaking idea that we can earn God's favor by praying or by believing, by obeying or by repenting. But the only way we get into his favor is by the free gift of his almighty grace.

It takes some of us a long time to understand that we don't deserve to be saved, and that nothing we do can make us deserving. We say to God, "I really am sorry for what I've done. I really am sick of myself." If only this were true! We have to become sick to death of ourselves, even to the point of despair, even to the point where we can do nothing. Then we will be in the exact right state for receiving his overflowing grace. "In him we have redemption through his blood, the forgiveness of sins, in accordance with the riches of God's grace" (Ephesians 1:7).

Think of what God's forgiveness means: it means he forgets away all our sins. Forgetting, in the human mind, may be a defect; in the divine mind it is an attribute. God illustrates it through vibrant images drawn from his creation: "As far as the east is from the west, so far has he removed our transgressions from us" (Psalm 103:12). "I have swept away your offenses like a cloud, your sins like the morning mist" (Isaiah 44:22).

When we think of forgetting in human terms, we place limits on God's grace that don't exist. His overflowing grace never ends. When God forgets our sins, he forgets them completely: "Though your sins are like scarlet, they shall be as white as snow; though they are red as crimson, they shall be like wool" (Isaiah 1:18). This is the grace of God's forgetting.

Why Can't I Follow Now?

Peter asked, "Lord, why can't I follow you now?"

JOHN 13:37

There are times when we can't do what we want, and we don't understand why. When this happens, *wait*. It is God who brings these blank spaces into our lives, and it is God who must fill them.

A blank space might come before we are sanctified, to teach us what sanctification means. Or it might come after, to teach us what service means. Whatever the reason, we must not try to fill it on our own. Never run before God's guidance. If there is the slightest doubt, then he is not guiding. Whenever there is doubt, *don't*.

Sometimes, we have a clear picture of an outcome God wants for us—the end of a certain friendship or business relationship, for example—but we are not sure about how God wants to accomplish it. If it isn't clear that God wishes *us* to act, we must wait. If we act impulsively, on a feeling, we will end up causing difficulties that could take years to put right. Wait for God, and he will accomplish the task without any heartbreak or disappointment.

In John 13, Peter doesn't want to wait. "I will lay down my life for you," he declares to Jesus (v. 37). It's an honest declaration, but an ignorant one: Peter doesn't know himself as Jesus does. "Jesus answered . . . 'Before the rooster crows, you will disown me three times!'" (v. 38). The feeling Peter wants to act on, his natural devotion to Jesus, is a good one. But Jesus wants him to act on something else—not devotion but discipleship. He uses the blank space, the "not now," to discipline Peter and bring about the thing Peter wants in the proper way and at the proper time.

Not Now, but Later

Where I am going, you cannot follow now, but you will follow later.

JOHN 13:36

When Peter first encountered Jesus, he was fascinated. Jesus said, "Follow me," and Peter went easily. Then he denied Jesus three times, his heart broke, and fascination turned to shame. When Jesus called to him again, Peter could go only because he'd received the Holy Spirit. The first time Peter followed, there was nothing mystical about it. The second was based on a supernatural change, an internal martyrdom made possible by the Spirit (John 21:18).

Between these two moments, Peter denied Jesus with oaths and curses. He came to the limits of himself, the end of his human power. Destitute and empty, realizing he could no longer trust himself, he was finally ready to receive the gift of the Spirit. "[Jesus] breathed on them and said, 'Receive the Holy Spirit'" (20:22). Now, when Peter looked to Jesus, all he saw was Jesus: not the dreams that had enchanted him before, not a vision of himself playing the devoted follower. God had changed Peter, awakening shame and self-knowledge inside him. Yet even these changes Peter knew not to count on. He'd learned to count only on a person—on Jesus himself—and on the Spirit he gives.

"Receive the Holy Spirit": it is an invasion, one that cannot happen until we come to the end of ourselves. We must come to this end not just in our imaginations but *really*. When we do, we realize that, in fact, we never did have any power of our own. That's why all our vows and resolutions ended in failure.

Now, on the other side of that failure, we see clearly. Only one star shines in our sky—our lodestar, Jesus Christ.

Worship

He . . . pitched his tent, with Bethel on the west and Ai
on the east. There he built an altar to the LORD.

GENESIS 12:8

Bethel is the symbol of communion with God; Ai is the symbol of
the world. Abraham pitched his tent between the two, knowing that
the value of his public activity for God depended on the moments of
profound private communion spent with him.

The two things—private worship and public work—went together
in Abraham's life, just as they did in the life of Christ. Too many of us
think that in order to worship we have to drop out of our everyday lives,
to flee Ai and go deep into Bethel, that quiet fortress where nothing and
no one can disturb us.

This way of thinking may be a trap. There is always time to worship,
no matter where we are or what we're doing. Rush is wrong every time.
Instead of jumping around like spiritual frogs, from working to waiting
to worshipping, we should strive to live as Jesus did: unhurrying and
unyielding, his entire existence an act of worship.

Worship is giving God the best he has given you. Be careful what you
do with the best you have. If you try to keep a blessing for yourself, it
will turn into spiritual rot, just as the manna rotted when the Israelites
hoarded it (Exodus 16). Offer it back to God as a love gift, in a deliberate
act of worship, and he will make it a blessing to others.

Intimate with Jesus

Jesus answered: "Don't you know me, Philip?"

JOHN 14:9

Jesus's words to Philip weren't said with criticism, or even with surprise. They were an invitation: Jesus wanted Philip to embrace a more intimate relationship with him.

Before Pentecost, the disciples knew Jesus as someone who gave them power to conquer demons and start a revival (Luke 10:18–20). The intimacy they felt with him was wonderful. But there was a much closer intimacy to come. Jesus said, "I have called you friends" (John 15:15). Friendship—true friendship—is rare on earth. It involves two people identifying with each other in thought and heart and spirit. Friendship with Jesus is the whole point of spiritual discipline, yet it is often the last thing we actually seek. We receive his blessings and know his word, but do we know him?

Jesus said, "It is for your good that I am going away" (16:7). He went so that he could lead his friends to ever greater heights and purposes. It is a joy to Jesus when we follow, when we move toward closer intimacy with him. The result is always abundance: "I am the vine; you are the branches. If you remain in me and I in you, you will bear much fruit" (15:5).

When we are intimate with Jesus, we are never lonely, never need sympathy. We can give tirelessly, pouring ourselves out. The impression we leave behind is never of ourselves, only of the strong, calm sanity of our Lord, a sign that our souls have been entirely satisfied by him.

Does My Sacrifice Live?

Abraham built an altar there and . . . bound his son Isaac.

GENESIS 22:9

Abraham's intentions in offering his son to God were good, but it was not the offering God wanted. "Do not lay a hand on the boy," the angel of the Lord told Abraham. "Do not do anything to him. Now I know that you fear God, because you have not withheld from me your son" (Genesis 22:12). God didn't want Isaac's death; he wanted Abraham's life.

We make a version of Abraham's mistake. We think that the ultimate thing God wants from us is the sacrifice of death. What God wants from us is the sacrifice *through* death that enables us to do what Jesus did: sacrifice our lives. The idea isn't "I am willing to go to death with Jesus," but "I am willing to be identified with Jesus's death so that I may sacrifice my life to God." Nowhere in Scripture does God ask us to give things up simply for the sake of giving them up. He asks us to give things up for the sake of the only thing worth having: a life with him.

God disciplined Abraham to show him the error of his belief, and the same discipline goes on in our lives. The goal is to loosen the ties that constrict the life of Christ in us, so that we can enter into a relationship with him. We may be challenged and disciplined until we finally understand: it is of no value to God to give him our lives for death. He wants us to be a *living* sacrifice, to let him have all our vibrant, vital powers. This is the offering that is acceptable to God.

Where God Can Go

May your whole spirit, soul and body be kept blameless.

1 THESSALONIANS 5:23

Paul's prayer for the Thessalonians, that they be kept blameless in their *whole* spirit, soul, and body, is a prayer that can only be answered through the great mystical work of the Holy Spirit.

Far beneath the surface of our personality lies a shadowy region we ourselves can't get at. This is where our deepest fears and motivations are found, those unconscious forces we haven't chosen and can't control. If we are to be made blameless here, we need the Spirit to seek us out: "You have searched me, LORD, and you know me," writes David in Psalm 139:1. "Where can I go from your Spirit? Where can I flee from your presence?" (v. 7).

The psalm is a testimony to God's omnipresence and eternity, his *everywhereness* and *alwaysness*. David is saying, "You are the God of the early mornings and the late-at-nights, the God of the mountain peaks and of the sea. But, my God, my soul has further horizons than the early mornings, deeper darknesses than the night, higher peaks than any mountain, greater depths than any sea. You who are God of all these things, be my God. There are motives I cannot understand, dreams I cannot grasp. Please, Lord, search them out."

Do we believe that God can garrison our imagination far beyond where we can go? As the ancient Romans sent garrisons of soldiers beyond the reaches of their empire, so God sends the Spirit to the outer limits of our soul. It is only when we are garrisoned by God in this way that we are made blameless. Blameless does not mean perfection but preserved in unspotted integrity, undeserving of censure in God's sight, until Jesus comes.

The Opened Sight

I am sending you to them to open their eyes and turn them from
darkness to light . . . so that they may receive forgiveness of sins
and a place among those who are sanctified by faith in me.

ACTS 26:17–18

To open their eyes . . . so that they may receive. This is the Bible's clearest
statement of where the disciple's work begins and ends. As disciples of
Jesus, we have a responsibility to open people's eyes to the gospel, to help
them turn toward the light. But this is only the work of conversion, not
of salvation. Conversion is the effort of a roused human being. Salvation
requires *receiving* something—not from another person but from God
himself. This is the first mighty work of grace: "That they may receive
forgiveness of sins."

When someone fails in personal Christian experience, it is nearly
always because they've never received anything. They've opened their
eyes, but they haven't accepted God's gifts. They may make vows and
promises, they may swear to walk in the light as God is in the light,
they may even succeed for a time, but none of this is salvation. Salvation
means that we have been brought, humble and open, to the place where
we are able to receive. The only sign that a person is saved is that they
have received the gift Jesus Christ bought for them on the cross.

"A place among those who are sanctified by faith in me." Sanctification
is the second mighty work of grace, God's second great gift to us. In
receiving the Holy Spirit, the reborn soul deliberately gives up its right
to itself, turns itself over to Jesus, and identifies entirely with God's will.
To be born again in the Spirit is to know beyond a doubt that it is only
through God's generosity that we are saved, not through any decision of
our own.

What My Obedience to God Costs Others

They seized Simon from Cyrene . . . and put the cross
on him and made him carry it behind Jesus.

LUKE 23:26

If we obey God, it is going to cost other people more than it costs us. We delight in obeying our Lord because we are in love with him. But this means that his plans come first in our lives, not the plans of other people. If the people around us do not love him, they may accuse us of indifference or selfishness. They may taunt us: "You call this Christianity?"

It isn't indifference or independence that makes us act as we do. Many of us would probably prefer to be independent, to carry the burden of our obedience alone, never asking anyone for anything. We must learn that to obey is to be swept up in God's *universal* purposes. His purpose for other people may be that they help us in his work, as Simon of Cyrene helped Jesus with the cross, or as Susanna offered him material support (Luke 8:2–3). To refuse help like this is to let our pride win out.

Are we going to remain loyal to God and go through the humiliation of depending on others? Or are we going to say, "I will not cause other people to suffer. I will not cost them anything"? Beware of the inclination to dictate to God what you will allow to happen if you obey him.

We can disobey God if we choose; we can prevent other people from suffering. Our disobedience will bring immediate relief. But it will hurt our Lord and, in the long run, fail to help anyone: God has already thought about the consequences of our obedience. If we obey, *he*—not we—will take care of everyone involved. We need only to let him.

Our Solitude with God

When he was alone with his own disciples, he explained everything.

MARK 4:34

Jesus doesn't get us alone and explain things to us all the time; he explains them as we become able to understand. Other people's lives are parables: they show us certain truths, but they do not walk the path for us. God is making us spell out our own souls, so that we may come to our understanding honestly, through our own experience.

God's ultimate aim, in asking us to do this work, is to shape us for his purposes. It is slow work, so slow that it takes him all of time and eternity to accomplish it. We must let him guide us through all the nooks and crannies of our characters. It is amazing how ignorant we are about ourselves! We don't recognize envy when it is inside us, or laziness, or pride. Jesus reveals these things to us. He reveals everything we've been hiding before his grace began to work. How many of us have learned to look in with courage?

We have to get rid of the idea that we understand ourselves: it is the last bit of conceitedness to go. Only God understands us. If we ever get a glimpse of what we are like in his sight, we will never again say, "Oh, I am so unworthy," because we will *know* we are, beyond having to say it. As long as we aren't quite sure, God will keep cornering us until he gets us alone. He'll wound our pride, take us to the limits of our intelligence, break our hearts. He'll show us where we have loved unwisely, or too much.

Only then, when we are truly cornered and alone with him, will he begin to explain.

God's Solitude with Us

Come with me by yourselves to a quiet place.

MARK 6:31

When God gets us alone—isolating us through sickness, heartbreak, or disappointment, through affliction, temptation, or unrequited love—when he gets us totally alone and we are so bewildered that we cannot ask him even one question, this is when he begins to teach us.

Most of the time, we are not alone with God in this way: it's why he must produce a crisis. We spend our lives distracted by fussy little worries about our work or our health or what other people are doing. Jesus can explain nothing to us until we learn to quiet our minds and leave others alone. If I am walking with him, the only thing he intends me to see clearly is how he is dealing with *my* soul. We think we understand other people's situations; then God shows us our own hearts, and we see that there are whole regions of stubbornness and ignorance inside us that we cannot access on our own. Only the Holy Spirit can reach these places.

If God has gotten you alone right now, if you are feeling isolated and bewildered, turn to the Spirit he has placed inside. It is the fine art of the Holy Spirit to be alone with God; it is a purpose of the Holy Spirit to guide and instruct: "The Holy Spirit, whom the Father will send in my name, will teach you all things" (John 14:26). Remember that God has not *left* you alone; he has *gotten* you alone *with him*. Go with God to a quiet place, and his Spirit will teach you all you need to know.

Called by God

I heard the voice of the Lord saying, "Whom shall I send? And
who will go for us?" And I said, "Here am I. Send me!"

ISAIAH 6:8

God didn't call Isaiah by name; he called for anyone willing to go. Isaiah simply heard and answered.

The call of God isn't reserved for a special few; it's for everyone. Whether or not we hear it depends on us. Are our ears open? Is our temperament in line with Christ's? "For many are invited, but few are chosen," Jesus said (Matthew 22:14). He meant that few *prove* themselves chosen. Chosen ones are those who, through Jesus Christ, have come into a relationship with God that has changed their temperament and opened their ears. All the time, they hear God asking, "Whom shall I send?"

God's call leaves us free to answer or not to answer. When Isaiah answered the call, it wasn't because God commanded him to. Isaiah was in God's presence and, when the call came, realized that there was nothing for him to do but to answer, consciously and freely, "Send me."

We have to get rid of the idea that if God really wants us to do something, he will come at us with force or pleading. When Jesus called the disciples, there was no irresistible compulsion from the outside. Instead, Jesus came with a quiet, passionate insistence, speaking to men who were wide awake, with all their powers and faculties intact. If we let the Spirit bring us face-to-face with God, we too will hear what Isaiah heard—"Whom shall I send?"—and we will say, in perfect freedom, "Here am I. Send me."

Buried with Him

We were therefore buried with him through baptism into
death in order that . . . we too may live a new life.

ROMANS 6:4

No one enters into the experience of entire sanctification without going
through the burial of the old life. If this crisis has never taken place,
if you've never put your old life to death, sanctification is nothing more
than a vision. It is a death followed by one resurrection—a resurrection
into the life of Jesus Christ. Nothing can upset such a life. It is one with
God for one purpose: to be a witness to him.

Have you come to your last days *really*? You may have come to them
many times in your thoughts and dreams; you may have grown excited
at the thought of being baptized into death with your Lord. But have
you actually done it? You cannot die in excitement. Death means you
stop being, stop striving. Do you agree with God to stop being the kind
of striving, eager Christian you've been up to now? We circle the cem-
etery all the time, refusing to actually go to our deaths.

Are you ready to be buried with Christ, or are you playing the fool
with your soul? Is there a moment you can identify as your last? Can
you go back to it in your memory and say, with a chastened and grateful
spirit, "That was when I made an agreement with God"?

"It is God's will that you should be sanctified" (1 Thessalonians 4:3).
When you realize that sanctification is what God wants, you will enter
into death naturally. Are you willing to do it now? Do you agree with
God that this day will be your last? The moment of agreement depends
on you.

The Call of God

I heard the voice of the Lord saying, "Whom shall I send?"

ISAIAH 6:8

What does the call of God sound like? There is the call of the sea, the call of the mountains, the call of the great ice barriers. These are calls heard only by the few—by those who have the sea or the mountains or the ice in their blood. So it is with the call of God. His call is the expression of his nature, and only those with the same nature inside them can hear it.

Have we ever heard God calling? His call always comes intimately, through the circumstances of our lives. There is no point asking anyone else about these circumstances; they are strands of our existence that God has woven specially for us.

It is easy—too easy—to miss the call. We have to maintain the profound relationship between our soul and God if we are to hear it. Isaiah was able to hear because, after the tremendous crisis he had been through, his soul, open and raw, was tuned in to God.

Most of us are tuned in only to ourselves; we hear nothing of what God is saying. I have to realize that the call of God is not an echo of my own nature. My likes and dislikes are not part of it. Neither is my temperament. As long as I place concern for myself at the center of my life, all I'll hear are my own thoughts, echoing back at me.

To be brought into an intimate conversation with God is to be profoundly changed. It is to see with our eyes, hear with our ears, and understand with our hearts all that God is saying (Isaiah 6:10).

God's Nature and Ours

But when God . . . was pleased to reveal his Son in me so
that I might preach him among the Gentiles . . .

GALATIANS 1:15–16

If the call of God is an expression of his nature, and not our own, how are we to answer it? Paul writes that he went out to preach the gospel when God called. The call was God's; the preaching was Paul's interpretation of it, an action fitted to Paul's own nature. Paul had always been able to preach, but now, having received the Holy Spirit, he began to use his gift for God's purposes.

This is what service means: God's nature awakening and filtering through our own. God's own nature is supernatural, but our acts of service to him are always part of our natural lives. We may be called to serve him in big ways or in small, through the seemingly unimportant tasks that fill our days. The size of the act doesn't matter. If we perform it as an act of service, it becomes a sacramental expression. To serve God is the deliberate love gift of a nature that has heard his call.

If I have received God's nature, if the Holy Spirit dwells inside me, I will hear the most beautiful echo when God calls, the voice from outside resounding on the inside, the two joining together to help me do his work. When the life of Jesus is revealed in me in this way, I will serve God's purposes all the time, pouring myself out in superabounding devotion to him.

Unbribed Devotion

When a Samaritan woman came to draw water, Jesus
said to her, "Will you give me a drink?"

JOHN 4:7

When Jesus asked the Samaritan woman for water, he indicated the
proper form our devotion should take. How many of us spend our
lives begging Jesus to satisfy our thirst, when we should be satisfying him?
To be a witness for the Lord is to lead a life of unsullied, uncompromising, and unbribed devotion. It is to make ourselves a satisfaction to him
wherever he places us.

Beware of anything that competes with loyalty to Jesus Christ. Sometimes, the greatest competitor of devotion to Jesus is service for him.
Instead of losing ourselves in love for our Savior, we busy ourselves with
work, allowing it to distract us from our relationship with him. Recall how
Jesus admonished Martha, as she rushed about doing chores while her
sister, Mary, sat devotedly at his feet: "Martha, Martha," Jesus said, "you
are worried and upset about many things, but few things are needed—or
indeed only one. Mary has chosen what is better" (Luke 10:41–42).

It is easier to serve than to be drunk with love and devotion. But the
one aim of the call of God is the satisfaction of God. It is not a call to
keep busy, or to rack up accomplishments, or to keep a running tally of
how many souls we've saved. All of that is God's concern, not ours, and
we must leave him to it. We are not called to battle for God but to be used
by God in *his* battles. Are we allowing ourselves to be used in this way?

Vision and Darkness

A thick and dreadful darkness came over him.

GENESIS 15:12

When God gives us a vision, he puts us, so to speak, in the shadow of his hand. There is a darkness that comes from too much light, and this is the time to listen. Thirteen years of silence passed between visions God sent Abraham, but in that time Abraham's selfishness and self-sufficiency were destroyed and he was transformed into the man God wanted him to be, a man worthy of being called the father of many nations (Genesis 17). Those years of silence were a time of discipline, not punishment.

Whenever God sends you a vision and darkness follows, *wait*. God is remaking you in the image of what he has shown you: "Let the one who walks in the dark, who has no light, trust in the name of the LORD and rely on their God" (Isaiah 50:10).

Am I trusting entirely in the name of the Lord, or is my confidence in myself and other people? Is it in books and prayers and ecstasies, or is it in God himself? The one thing for which we are all being disciplined is to know that God is real. Until we know this, the vision will not come to pass. After we know it, everything that seemed so real to us before—books and prayers, other people's words and actions—will become as shadows. Nothing can disturb the one who is built on God.

Are You Fresh for Everything?

No one can see the kingdom of God unless they are born again.

JOHN 3:3

Being born again of the Spirit is an unmistakable work of God, as mysterious as the wind, as surprising as God himself. We do not know where it begins; it is hidden away in the depths of our personal lives.

Being born again from above is a perennial, perpetual, and eternal beginning. It is a freshness all the time in thinking and talking and living, the continual surprise of the life of God. Sometimes, we are fresh for a prayer meeting, but not for cleaning boots! If this is the case, it's a sign that something isn't right between our souls and God. If we've ever found ourselves grumbling, "I *have* to do this thing or it will never get done," we've let staleness creep in.

Consider the moment you are in right now: Do you feel the spark of eternity, of life itself, lighting you from within? The spark never comes from our own efforts. Obedience keeps us in the light, but it doesn't fill us with vibrant, vital, untiring life. This can only come from the Spirit. To keep in touch with the Spirit within, we must jealously guard our relationship to God. Jesus prayed that we would be one as he and the Father are one—with absolutely nothing in between (John 17:21).

Keep every area of your life continually open to Jesus Christ. Don't pretend with him. Are you drawing on any other source than God himself? If you're depending upon anything but him, you will never know when he is gone. Being born of the Spirit means much more than we generally take it to mean. It gives us a new vision and keeps us absolutely fresh for everything, thanks to the perennial supply of the life of God.

What God Remembers

I remember the devotion of your youth.

JEREMIAH 2:2

Am I as spontaneously kind to God as I used to be, or am I only expecting God to be kind to me? Am I full of the sort of small, simple actions and thoughts that cheer his heart? Or am I constantly irritated, obsessed with the idea that things aren't going my way?

There is no joy in the soul that has forgotten what God loves and needs. Think on this: *God needs you.* Do you know that? It is a great thing. "Will you give me a drink?" Jesus asked the Samaritan woman, counting on the spontaneous spark of goodness and charity that might lead someone from a different people, a different tribe, to offer help (John 4:7). We too must act in spontaneous joy and love for his sake—the sake of his reputation with others.

Do I remember how it was in the beginning of my relationship with him? God does: "I remember the devotion of your youth." God remembers when I cared for nothing but him, when I had an extravagance of love for Jesus, when I would have gone anywhere, done anything, to prove my love.

Am I still so in love that I take no consideration for myself? Or have I grown calculating, always watching for the respect I think I deserve, weighing how much service I should give, asking if it's worth it?

Remember as God remembers. And if you find that he is not what he used to be—your soul's beloved—let it produce shame and humiliation. The shame will bring the goodly, godly sorrow that works repentance.

Where Am I Looking?

Look unto me, and be ye saved.

ISAIAH 45:22 KJV

The mind wanders, casting about. It worries over today and tomorrow, growing dizzy with its troubles and trials. These troubles vanish when we look to God, but we must truly *look*: to look means to concentrate fully on Jesus. This, in effect, is the teaching of the Sermon on the Mount: we must narrow all our interests until the attitude of our mind and heart and body is concentration on Jesus Christ (Matthew 5–7).

To look to God is to be saved. We have stories and ideas in our minds of great Christian saints and heroes. We think we must emulate their lives to be saved. But there is no salvation in emulation; it is not simple enough. "Look unto me, and be ye saved," says God. Not "you *will* be saved" but "you *are* saved." We get preoccupied and grumpy with God, and all the time he is saying, "Just look."

Concentrating on God is a great spiritual challenge. It is easier in times of trouble, when we desperately need him, than in times of peace and contentment. God's blessings absorb us, pulling us away in delighted distraction. We must not let them. Though a thousand wonderful things vie for our attention, we must learn to let them come and go, keeping our focus on God.

"Look unto me," says God. The moment you look, salvation *is*.

The Unveiled Face

And we all, who with unveiled faces contemplate the
Lord's glory, are being transformed into his image.

2 CORINTHIANS 3:18

The most remarkable characteristic of a Christian is the unveiled face.
Open and honest, hiding nothing, we stand before God so that our
lives may become a mirror of his. By being filled with the Spirit, we are
transformed. By standing unveiled before him, we become his mirror. It
is always easy to sense when someone has been beholding the glory of
the Lord. We can *feel* the Lord's own character, shining out from within.

The golden rule for the Christian life is this unfailing concentration on
God. If God requires it, we must be willing to set aside our concerns for
everything else—work, food, clothing, shelter, *everything*. The busyness
of modern life tends to draw our attention away from God, darkening the
mirror within. Usually, the thing that dirties the mirror is a "good" thing,
a worthy concern. It is the *good* that is the enemy of the *best*.

Let other things come and go as they may. Let other people criticize
as they will. But never let anything disturb the life that is hidden with
Christ in God. Never be hurried out of the relationship of abiding in
him. This is the one thing that tends to get pushed aside, and it is the one
thing that shouldn't. It is the toughest discipline we undergo as Christians: the discipline of keeping our focus on the glory of the Lord.

The Overmastering Relationship

I have appeared to you to appoint you as a servant and as a witness.

ACTS 26:16

Paul's vision on the road to Damascus was no passing dream. It was a vision that brought with it clear and emphatic instructions. Jesus told Paul that from now on Paul's whole life was to be mastered: it was to be subdued, to have no end, aim, or purpose except Christ's. *"I have appeared to you to appoint you as a servant."*

All of us, when we are born again, have visions of what Jesus wants us to be. The big thing we must learn is not to be disobedient to the vision; we must not say that it can't be attained. We think it can't be attained because our faith doesn't have the proper foundations. It isn't enough to believe that God has redeemed the world, or that the Holy Spirit can make all that Jesus did come alive in us. We must have the basis of a personal relationship with him. Paul wasn't given a script or a doctrine to proclaim; he was brought into a vivid, personal, overmastering relationship with Jesus Christ, and *on this basis* he became a witness.

We too must have as the foundation of our faith a personal relationship with Jesus. This is the only way our vision will be attained, and the only way we'll succeed in obeying it. Verse 16 is immensely commanding: "to appoint you as a servant and as a witness." There is nothing there apart from a personal relationship.

Paul was devoted to a person, not a cause. He was absolutely Jesus Christ's. He saw nothing else; he lived for nothing else. "For I resolved to know nothing while I was with you except Jesus Christ and him crucified" (1 Corinthians 2:2).

Leave Room for God

But when it pleased God . . .

GALATIANS 1:15 KJV

Have you learned how to leave space for God—to give him a little elbow room to work in your life? Too often, as we go about making our plans, we forget to leave a place for God to come in as he chooses. We say that this or that will happen, but none of our predictions leave room for the element of divine surprise.

Would we be shocked if God came into our meetings, our prayers, or our preaching in a way we'd never expected? However well we think we know God, we can never know exactly what he'll do. What we *can* know is that, when it pleases him, he will break in. This is the great lesson to learn—that at any minute God may arrive. We tend to overlook this element of surprise, and yet God never works in any other way.

Keep in constant, intimate contact with God, so that his surprising power may break through at any time and any place. Always be in a state of expectancy, and remember to leave room. Do not look for God to come in any particular way, but do look for him.

Look Again and Consecrate

If that is how God clothes the grass of the field . . .
will he not much more clothe you?

MATTHEW 6:30

A simple message is always a puzzle to those who aren't simple. What Jesus is saying here is "God looks after those who seek his kingdom, so seek and don't worry about anything else." But we'll never be able to take this message to heart if we don't possess Jesus's own simplicity.

To be simple is to concentrate on our relationship with him. We slip out of spiritual communion when we complicate things, worrying and overthinking and insisting we know better than God. We get lost in the cares of the world, and we forget the promise of "much more." Jesus compares us to the "birds of the air" (Matthew 6:26): their only goal is to obey the principle of life inside them. What principle is inside us? Jesus says that if we are rightly related to him, obeying the Spirit inside, God will look after our "feathers."

To be simple is to grow where we are planted. "See how the flowers of the field grow," Jesus says (v. 28). Many of us refuse to grow where we're planted, and the result is that we never take root, never blossom fully. Jesus says that we shouldn't go running after the things we think we need. If we obey the life God has given us, he will look after the rest.

To be simple is to consecrate each moment to God. Consecration involves setting ourselves aside for one particular thing—giving it our attention, dedicating our actions to it. We can't consecrate ourselves to God once and be done with it. We must consecrate continually, each moment and every action. If we do, we will find ourselves absolutely free: free to do God's work, free to live lives of amazing simplicity, free to set aside confusion, angst, and worry.

Look Again and Think

Do not worry about your life.

MATTHEW 6:25

How easy following this command would be if we could just decide, once and for all, to stop worrying about the world and its demands; if, having pledged ourselves to Jesus, we could just forget about the things that used to obsess us. But answering the call is never this easy. The cares of this world, the deceitfulness of riches, the pull of desire and hunger and lust—these are recurring tides, always lapping at our shores. If we don't allow the Spirit of God to rise up against them, they'll come flooding in.

Jesus is telling us to be careful about one thing only: our relationship to him. Common sense shouts that this is ridiculous, that we must think about what we're going to eat and drink and wear. Jesus says we must not. Beware of thinking that Jesus's words don't apply to your particular circumstances, that he doesn't understand what you're going through right now. Jesus understands your circumstances better than you do, and he says you must not make these things the central concern of your life. Whenever there's a competition, put your relationship to God first.

"Each day has enough trouble of its own" (Matthew 6:34). How much trouble has begun to threaten you today? What mean little imps have been looking in and saying, "What are you going to do next month, next summer, next year?" "Do not be anxious," Paul tells us (Philippians 4:6). Look again, and think, drawing your awareness to the "much more" of your heavenly Father: "Will he not much more clothe you—you of little faith?" (Matthew 6:30).

Our Way or His?

Saul, Saul, why do you persecute me?

ACTS 26:14

Are we determined to serve God in our own way, or in his? Until we undergo the baptism by fire of the Holy Spirit, we will always be tempted to put our own ambitions and interests first. We won't understand that our self-will and stubbornness stab Jesus, that our insistence on our own dignity and rightness hurts him. Every time we stand on our right to ourselves and insist that this is what we intend to do, we persecute our Lord.

When we realize what we've been doing, it is the most crushing thing. We see that we've been lying, see that every time we went out into the world with the Lord's name on our lips and selfishness in our hearts, we were persecuting Christ. We were preaching sanctification while exhibiting the spirit of Satan.

Is the word of God alive and true in me as I hand it on to you, or does my life prove the lie of what I say? That is the question we must ask ourselves. The Spirit of Jesus is conscious of one thing only: a perfect oneness with the Father. All we do should be founded on this oneness, not a prideful determination to "be godly." "Learn from me," Jesus said, "I am gentle and humble in heart" (Matthew 11:29). If we are gentle and humble, it means that we can be easily taken advantage of, easily snubbed, and easily ignored. But if we submit to this treatment for his sake, we will prevent Jesus Christ being persecuted.

The Unmistakable Voice of God

Who are you, Lord?

ACTS 26:15

Has the voice of God come to you directly? If it has, you cannot mistake the intimate insistence with which it has spoken. It comes to you in the language you know best, not through your ears but through your circumstances.

When we have gone astray, when we have grown too sure of ourselves, God has to come in and set us right. He has to destroy our determined confidence in our own convictions. In these moments, his voice is overwhelming. He speaks to us as he spoke to Isaiah, with a "strong hand," revealing to us the depths of our ignorance (Isaiah 8:11). He tells us that we've been serving Jesus in a spirit that is not his, pushing his message in the spirit of the devil. The words we've been speaking might have *sounded* right, but our spirit was that of the enemy: "If I speak in the tongues of men or of angels, but do not have love, I am only a resounding gong or a clanging cymbal" (1 Corinthians 13:1).

There is no escape when our Lord speaks. I must take his rebuke to heart: "Ye know not what manner of spirit ye are of" (Luke 9:55 KJV). Have I been persecuting Jesus by a zealous determination to serve him in my own way? To do God's work in the Spirit of Jesus is to have the humble and gentle Spirit kindled inside me. If instead I am filled with self-satisfaction or a grim sense of having "done my duty," I know that in fact I have *not* done it. We imagine that anything unpleasant is our duty! Is that at all like the Spirit of the Lord? "I delight to do thy will, O my God" (Psalm 40:8 KJV).

The Dilemma of Obedience

Samuel . . . was afraid to tell Eli the vision.

1 SAMUEL 3:15

When God speaks, it is never startling, seldom obvious. He comes to us in our circumstances, moving so subtly and mysteriously through our lives that we wonder, "Is that God's voice?" Isaiah said that God spoke to him with a "strong hand"—the all-encompassing hand of circumstance, holding and guiding him (Isaiah 8:11). Nothing touches our lives that God isn't speaking through.

What do we see in our own circumstances? The hand of God, or simply accidents? When we begin to understand that there are no accidents, that all is God, life begins to change. We begin to say, "Speak, Lord," and to listen. We begin to realize that difficulty does more than discipline us; it brings us to the place where, attentive and hungry, we say, "Speak, Lord." Get into the habit of saying, "Speak, Lord," and life becomes a romance.

Perhaps we've already heard the call, but we were afraid to answer, fearing that answering would hurt someone we love. God called to Samuel, and Samuel hesitated, wanting to protect Eli. But Eli knew that Samuel must obey; if he did not, he would turn himself into an amateur providence. As cruel as it may seem, we must not prevent the gouging out of the eye, the cutting off of the hand (Matthew 5:29–30). We too are circumstances God is using to speak to others.

Every time circumstances press, say, "Speak, Lord," and make time to listen. As you listen, your ears grow sharp, until, like Jesus, you hear God all the time.

Abiding Reality

Set apart for the gospel of God . . .

ROMANS 1:1

The one abiding reality is the gospel of God. Other things may be real; the gospel is reality itself. We are brought into this reality through the redemption; the cross is our bridge and our entry point. Our access to it is a gift, purchased for us by Jesus Christ. We cannot get at it through any action of our own.

This is a crucial thing for us to understand. The reason God calls us is so that we will proclaim his gospel. God isn't asking us to go out and play the part of holy men or holy women. Personal holiness is an effect, not a cause. If we place our faith in our own holiness, we will stumble when the test comes.

In Romans 1, Paul doesn't say that *he* set himself apart from his previous life; he says that *God* set him apart. Paul doesn't need to take the credit. He isn't hypersensitive about his character; he's unconscious of it, recklessly abandoned to God. As long as our eyes are fixed on our own holiness, rather than Christ's, we'll never get to the reality of redemption. It's as though we're asking God to keep us away from the ruggedness of human life as it is, away from the filth and decay and corruption and mess, so that we can spend time in our own perfectly ordered company and be made more desirable in our own eyes.

If this is what we want, it's a sign that we ourselves are still unreal—the gospel hasn't begun to touch us. When it does, when we enter into reality, then we are able to abandon all to God.

The Call of God

Christ did not send me to baptize, but to preach the gospel.

1 CORINTHIANS 1:17

I f we are going to preach the gospel, we need to be clear about what the gospel *is*. In his letters to the Corinthians, Paul says that the gospel—the message God has called on him to deliver—is the reality of redemption in our Lord Jesus Christ. The gospel isn't Paul's personal transformation or experience; it isn't his salvation or sanctification. Paul shares his personal story, but only as an illustration: certain things happened to Paul because of the redemption, but they were not the ultimate reason for it. The ultimate reason Jesus suffered in redemption was to redeem the whole world and place it unimpaired and rehabilitated before the throne of God. This is the gospel, and the only thing we are commissioned to preach.

The difference between Jesus's act of redemption and our personal holiness is stark: one is cause and the other effect. When we preach, we must be careful where we place the emphasis. Are we placing it on Jesus, or on ourselves? Are we lifting up his holiness, or our own?

When we truly understand the reality of the gospel, we will stop bothering God with questions about ourselves. Imagine, if God were human, how heartsick and tired he would be, listening to the constant requests for our salvation and sanctification! We trouble him day and night, when we should be thanking him. Paul welcomed heartbreak, disillusionment, and tribulation for one reason only: they kept him in unmoved devotion to the gospel of God.

The Constraint of the Call

Woe to me if I do not preach the gospel!

1 CORINTHIANS 9:16

Have you been called to preach the gospel as a disciple of Jesus Christ? If you have, beware of turning a deaf ear. The call to discipleship is a special kind of call. Everyone who is saved is called to testify to their salvation, but there is nothing easier than being saved. Salvation is God's sovereign work; all we have to do is turn to him. "Turn to me and be saved" (Isaiah 45:22). Our Lord never says that the conditions of discipleship are the same as the conditions of salvation. We are condemned to salvation through the cross of Jesus Christ, but discipleship has an option with it: "Whoever *wants* to be my disciple must deny themselves and take up their cross daily and follow me" (Luke 9:23).

To become a disciple is to be made broken bread and poured-out wine in Jesus's hands; it is to experience the pain of being constrained. In 1 Corinthians 9:16, Paul describes the distress that would seize him if he tried to break free. Having accepted the conditions of discipleship, he is now "set apart for the gospel," entirely kept and bound for God (Romans 1:1).

To lead a set-apart life is to suffer agonies worthy of the name *disciple*. Every personal ambition is nipped in the bud; every personal desire is erased; every perspective apart from God's is blotted out. Discipleship is not for everyone. But if you have felt God grip you for it, beware: woe be to the soul who puts a foot in any other direction once the call has come.

The Demand of the Call

We have become the scum of the earth, the garbage of the world.

1 CORINTHIANS 4:13

Paul's words here are not an exaggeration. If they are not true for us, it's because we refuse to allow ourselves to become garbage. Our preference for the finer things of the world, and for our own place among them, prevents us from being "set apart for the gospel" in the way Paul describes (Romans 1:1). When he writes of using his own flesh to "fill up . . . what is still lacking in regard to Christ's afflictions," he means being willing to put himself, in person, anywhere Christ's gospel is needed (Colossians 1:24).

"Do not be surprised at the fiery ordeal that has come on you to test you, as though something strange were happening" (1 Peter 4:12). If we do find the things we encounter strange, it's because we're cowardly and pretentious. We allow our worldly affinities and aspirations to keep us out of the muck: "I won't stoop," we say. "I won't bend." God won't force us. If we want, we can refuse to let Jesus count us as one of his servants.

A servant of Jesus is someone who is willing to become a martyr for the gospel. Martyrdom is a calling that lies beyond mere morality. When a merely moral man or woman comes in contact with baseness and immorality and treachery, they instinctively recoil. What they've seen is so desperately offensive to their sense of human goodness that their heart shuts up in despair.

But the marvel of the redemptive reality of God is that his love is bottomless: the worst and vilest can never exhaust it. Paul doesn't say that God set him apart in order to make him a shining example. It was, Paul writes, "to reveal his Son in me" (Galatians 1:16).

In God's Grip

For Christ's love compels us.

2 CORINTHIANS 5:14

When Paul says that he is compelled by Christ's love, he means that he is overruled, overmastered, held by an iron grip. Most of us have no idea what it means to be held in the grip of God's love. We are held only by our experience. The one thing that held Paul was love. Whenever you see someone held like this, you know there is nothing standing in the way of the Spirit of God.

For some time after we are saved, our testimony tends to focus on what God has done for us. The baptism of the Holy Spirit takes our focus off ourselves, and places it on Jesus Christ. Jesus said, "You will be my witnesses" (Acts 1:8). He didn't say "witnesses to what I have done for you." It isn't wrong to share personal testimony, but Christ wants us to pass on to a deeper, more profound kind of witness. He wants us to learn to view everything that happens to us as if it were happening to him—any praise we receive, any persecution we suffer. This is why we must be overruled by love and by the majesty of our Lord's personal power. If we aren't, we won't be able to stand for him.

Paul lived to persuade people of the judgment seat of God and the love of Christ. Some called him insane, but Paul didn't care. *He* understood the reason behind his actions: the love of Christ had him in its grip.

When we too are filled with this love, everything we do will give the impression of God's holiness and power, never our own. Then we will truly be witnesses, and our lives will bear wonderful fruit.

Are You Ready to Be Offered?

I am being poured out like a drink offering on the
sacrifice and service coming from your faith.

PHILIPPIANS 2:17

Are you ready to be offered, to become broken bread and poured-out wine in the hands of the Lord? Or are you full of hesitation, saying to yourself, "I'm not going to be offered up just yet. I'm not going to let God choose my work or the setting of my sacrifice. I'll only offer myself when the 'right' kind of people are watching, so they can congratulate me and say, 'Well done'"?

It's one thing to go about God's business unnoticed, walking a lonely path and filled with dignified heroism; it's quite another to become a doormat under other people's feet. Sometimes, the role God wants you to play is the lowly role. He wants to teach you to say, "I know how to be humbled."

Are you ready to be offered up like this? To be just a drop in the bucket, so hopelessly insignificant that no one even thinks of you in connection to the deeds you've done? Are you willing to spend and be spent, not seeking to *be* served but to serve (Matthew 20:28)?

Some saints are too holy for menial work. Are you one of them? Or will you decide that nothing God gives you to do is beneath you?

Are You Ready to Be Offered?

For I am already being poured out like a drink offering.

2 TIMOTHY 4:6

To be ready to be offered is a question of will, not feelings. If we always wait to act until we feel like it, we might never do anything at all. But if we take the initiative and decide to act, exerting our will, if we tell God that we are ready to be offered and that we will accept the consequences, whatever they may be, we will find that no matter what he asks, we are able to do it without complaint.

God puts each of us through crises we must face alone. These are trials intended just for us; no one else can help us with them. But if we prepare for these challenges internally first—if we say, "I *will* meet this challenge, no matter what"—then we'll be able to rise to the challenge when it actually comes, taking no thought for the cost to ourselves. If we don't make this kind of determined, private agreement with God in advance, we'll end up falling into self-pity when difficulty arises.

"Bind the sacrifice with cords, even unto the horns of the altar" (Psalm 118:27 KJV). The altar represents the purifying fire, the fire that burns away every attachment God has not chosen for us, every connection that isn't a connection to him. *We* don't choose what gets burned away; God does. Our job is to bind the sacrifice, and to make sure we don't give in to self-pity when the fire starts. After we've traveled this way of fire, there is nothing that can oppress us or make us afraid. When crises come, we realize that things cannot touch us as they once did.

Tell God you are ready to be offered, and God will prove himself all you ever dreamed he was.

The Discipline of Dejection

But we had hoped that he was the one who was going to
redeem Israel. And what is more, it is the third day.

LUKE 24:21

The disappointment the disciples express in this verse points to an important truth: it's possible to have the facts right and to come to the wrong conclusion. The disciples had the facts right about Jesus, but they'd grown impatient and dejected, replacing bright hope with dashed hope and a sense that Jesus had failed them.

Spiritual dejection is always wrong and always our fault—not God's or anyone else's. Dejection is often a sign of physical sickness, and spiritually it is the same. Spiritual dejection springs from one of two sources: either I've satisfied a lust, or I haven't. To lust after something is to say, "I must have it at once." Spiritual lust makes us go to God with demands, instead of seeking God himself.

What have I been hoping God will do? Am I irritated that it's already the "third day" and he hasn't done it? It's easy to imagine that my feelings are justified; hasn't God promised to answer my prayers (Matthew 21:22)? Whenever I find myself reasoning like this, *insisting* that God answers prayer, I can be sure I'm offtrack.

We look for visions from heaven, for earthquakes and thunder that "prove" God's power, and we feel dejected when we don't see them. We never dream that God is in the people and things around us. If we do the duty that lies nearest, we will see him. One of the most amazing revelations comes when we learn that it is in the commonplace things that the deity of Jesus Christ is realized. When we understand this, we are filled with wonder, and the spirit of dejection fades away.

One with Him

May God himself, the God of peace, sanctify you through and through.

1 THESSALONIANS 5:23

When we pray to be sanctified, are we praying for the standard Paul sets here—the "through and through"? We take the term *sanctification* much too superficially. Sanctification means an intense narrowing of our earthly interests and an immense broadening of our interests in God. It means an intense concentration on God's point of view—every power of body, soul, and spirit bound and kept for him. Are we prepared to let God do his work in us? And when his work is done, are we prepared to set ourselves apart, as Jesus set himself apart?

God wants us to be sanctified entirely. The reason some of us haven't entered into the experience of entire sanctification is that we haven't understood the meaning of it from God's viewpoint: "For them I sanctify myself, that they too may be truly sanctified" (John 17:19). Sanctification means being made one with Jesus, so that the mindset which ruled him will also rule us. Are we prepared for what that will cost? It will cost everything that is not of God in us.

To be caught up in the swing of Paul's prayer, the "through and through," means asking God to make us as holy as he can make sinners saved by grace. Jesus prayed that we might be one with him as he is one with the Father (v. 21). The sanctified soul has one defining characteristic: a strong family resemblance to Jesus, a freedom from everything that doesn't resemble him. Are we prepared to embrace this freedom by setting ourselves apart? Will we agree to let Jesus make us one with him, as he is one with the Father?

Are You Spiritually Exhausted?

The everlasting God . . . does not faint or grow weary.

ISAIAH 40:28 ESV

When we are physically exhausted, it's as though all our strength and vitality have left us. Spiritual exhaustion is similar: we feel as though we've come to the end of our ability to be of service to God. This kind of tiredness never arises through sin, always through service, and it happens when we're getting our supply from the wrong source.

Jesus told Peter, "Feed my sheep" (John 21:17), but he didn't give Peter anything to feed them with. The nourishment was Peter himself. He had to be made broken bread and poured-out wine for souls who hadn't yet learned to draw directly on God. We must offer ourselves like this as well, because other souls must draw from us before they draw directly on the Lord. But we must be very careful about where we find our own nourishment. If we don't get it from God, before long we will be completely exhausted.

Have you betrayed yourself into exhaustion by the way you've been serving God? Continually go back to your motivations and examine the source of their power. If you find yourself saying, "Oh, God, I'm so exhausted," remember that he saved and sanctified you *in order to* exhaust you. Exhaust yourself in service for God, but remember to take your supply from him: "All my fountains are in you" (Psalm 87:7).

Is Your Imagination of God Starved?

Lift up your eyes and look to the heavens: Who created
all these? He who brings out the starry host one by
one and calls forth each of them by name.

ISAIAH 40:26

In Isaiah's day, God's people had starved their imaginations by looking
on the faces of idols. Isaiah told them to look to God, to the author
of everything created and imagined. He made them lift their eyes to the
heavens, so that they might begin to use their imaginations aright.

Nature to a child of God is sacramental. In every wind that blows,
in every night and every day, in every sign of the sky, in every blossom-
ing and withering of the earth, there is a real coming of God to us, if
we will only use our starved imaginations to realize it. If we learn to
associate ideas worthy of God with all that happens in nature—with the
sunrises and the sunsets, with the moon and the stars, with the changing
seasons—our imaginations will never be at the mercy of our impulses
but will always be at his service.

Is your imagination looking on the face of an idol? Is the idol yourself? Your work? Your experiences of salvation and sanctification? If your
imagination is God-starved, you will have no power when difficulties
arise. When you need strength, don't look to your own experience or
understanding; it is God you need. Go out of yourself—away from your
idols, away from everything that has been starving your imagination.
Take Isaiah's words to heart: lift your eyes to the heavens and deliberately
turn your mind to God.

Is Your Hope in God Faint and Dying?

Thou wilt keep him in perfect peace, whose mind is
stayed on thee: because he trusteth in thee.

ISAIAH 26:3 KJV

Is your imagination stayed on God, or is it starved? A starved imagination is one of the greatest sources of exhaustion in a disciple's life. To attain the perfect peace Isaiah describes, we must set our minds steadfastly on God, trusting entirely in him.

If you have never used your imagination to put yourself deliberately before God, begin to do it now. It is no use waiting for God to come to you: you must go to him, turning your gaze away from the faces of idols. Imagination is the greatest gift God has given us, and it ought to be devoted entirely to him. If you learn to bring every thought into captivity to the obedience of Christ, it will be one of the greatest assets to your faith when the time of trial comes, because your faith and the Spirit of God will work together.

"We have sinned, even as our ancestors did. . . . They did not remember your many kindnesses" (Psalm 106:6–7). If you find that your mind is not steadfastly set on God, if you cannot remember his kindness and love, drive a stake through the heart of your forgetfulness. Remember whose you are and whom you serve. If you do, your affection for God will increase tenfold, your imagination will be quick and enthusiastic, and your hope will be inexpressibly bright.

Must I Listen?

They stayed at a distance and said to Moses, "Speak to us yourself
and we will listen. But do not have God speak to us or we will die."

EXODUS 20:18–19

There are times when we're not consciously disobeying God; we're just
not paying attention. God has given us his commandments: there
they are, set down in Scripture, along with a clear directive that we should
follow them. "If you love me, keep my commands" (John 14:15). And
still, we look the other way. We don't do this out of willful disobedience.
We do it because we don't love and respect God.

"Speak to us yourself," the Israelites told Moses. "But do not have
God speak to us." We show God how little we love him when we prefer
to listen only to his servants. We'll listen to personal testimonies, but
we won't listen to God himself. Why are we so terrified of him speaking
directly to us? Because we know that if he does, we'll have a choice to
make: obey or disobey. If it's only a servant's voice we hear, we feel free
to disregard it. "Well, that's just your own idea," we say. "Even though I
don't deny it's probably God's truth."

Am I putting God in the humiliating position of having treated me
as his child, while I've been ignoring him? When I do finally listen, the
humiliation I've been putting on him comes back on me, and my delight at
hearing him is tempered by the shame of having shut him out for so long.

The Devotion of Listening

Then Samuel said, "Speak, for your servant is listening."

1 SAMUEL 3:10

A m I hearing what God is saying? Perhaps I've listened well to one of his commands, but I've turned a deaf ear to the rest. This is how I show God that I don't love or respect him: I act like I can't hear him, even though he is speaking to me clearly. Samuel deliberately turned his attention to God, and assured God that his ears were open.

Jesus said, "You are my friends if you do what I command" (John 15:14). Am I being a friend to the Lord, or am I disobeying his commands? If I'd been listening, I wouldn't have consciously disobeyed. Most of us don't care enough to listen. Our Lord might as well have said nothing at all.

The goal of my spiritual life is to be so closely identified with Jesus Christ that I always hear God and I *know* that he always hears me (John 17). When I am identified with the Lord like this, my ears are attuned to his voice at every moment and in every situation. A lily, a tree, the words of one of his servants: all may convey God's message. If I haven't cultivated this devotion of listening, his voice comes through to me only at certain times. Most of the time, caught up in serving or in my convictions, I pretend I'm too busy to listen. Serving is a good thing, but if it drowns out God's voice, I know my devotion is running in the wrong direction.

Have I heard God's voice today, or have I become deaf to him?

The Discipline of Darkness

What I tell you in the dark, speak in the daylight.

MATTHEW 10:27

At times, God puts us into the shadow of his hand, holding us in darkness so that we might be still and learn to listen. Songbirds are taught to sing in the dark; we are taught to hear our Lord.

Are you in the dark right now, confused about your circumstances or your life with God? If you are, keep quiet: darkness is the time to listen. If you talk in the dark, you will talk in the wrong mood. Don't consult other people about your problem; don't seek the answers in a book. Other people's voices and opinions will drown out what God is trying to tell you. Listen to God in the dark, and he will give you a precious message for someone else when you get back into the light.

After every time of darkness, there comes a mixture of delight and humiliation. There is delight at finally hearing God, and humiliation at how long it took to listen. "How slow I've been in understanding!" you'll say. "And yet, God has been saying it all these days and weeks." If you feel only delight, it is doubtful you have heard him at all.

Learn to welcome the humiliation as a gift: it is God's way of teaching you how to listen better in the future. If you do, you will develop the softness of heart that always hears God *now*.

Am I My Brother's Keeper?

For none of us lives for ourselves alone.

ROMANS 14:7

Has it ever dawned on you that you are spiritually responsible for other souls? If you ever find yourself turning away from God, even in private, watch out: you will cause harm to everyone around you. "There are many parts, but one body," Paul wrote. "If one part suffers, every part suffers with it" (1 Corinthians 12:20, 26).

If we care about our friends, families, and communities, we must set a close guard on our hearts and minds. To give in to physical selfishness, intellectual laziness, or spiritual stubbornness is to put everyone around us at risk. "But who is strong enough to meet a standard like that?" you say. Our strength comes from God, and God alone.

When Jesus called us to be his witnesses, he meant that we should spend every bit of our mental, moral, and spiritual energy for him (Acts 1:8). When we embrace this calling, we will find that we've been made entirely useless from every viewpoint but his. It takes time; we must be patient with ourselves. But we must also remember why we are here: not to be saved and sanctified but to give our all for his sake. This is how we say thank you to God for the unspeakable gift of our salvation.

Inspired Initiative

Wake up, sleeper, rise from the dead, and Christ will shine on you.

EPHESIANS 5:14

Not all initiative is inspired. "Just do it," people say. "Just get on with it." That is ordinary human initiative. But when the Spirit of God comes in and says, "Wake up, sleeper, rise from the dead," we find ourselves genuinely inspired and ready to act.

We all have visions and ideals when we are young, but sooner or later we find that we have no power to make them real. We give up on our dreams and let them die; we let our ideals wither away. Then God comes in with his miraculous power, and we find we are able to do the impossible.

A mistake we make is believing that, because God is capable of miracles, we don't need to put forth any effort of our own. When God says, "Rise from the dead," we have to get up; God will not lift us up. In Matthew 12, Jesus heals a man with a shriveled hand—but first, Jesus asks the man to reach out to him. "He said to the man, 'Stretch out your hand.' So he stretched it out and it was completely restored" (v. 13). As the man acted in faith, Jesus acted to help the man. The same principle holds true in our lives: Although God, in his infinite power, *could* give us a life of instant, effortless gratification, this is not his will for us. Instead, he asks us to extend ourselves to him as he extends himself to us.

If the Lord has extended the hand of spiritual initiative to you, reach out and take it. As soon as you do, you will find that the light of God's inspiration is yours: "And Christ will shine on you."

The Initiative against Discouragement

An angel touched him and said, "Get up and eat."

1 KINGS 19:5

When the angel came to Elijah, the prophet was in a terrible state, huddled under a bush in the wilderness, afraid and miserable and wanting to die: "'I have had enough, LORD,' he said. 'Take my life'" (1 Kings 19:4).

How did the angel respond? He didn't give Elijah a vision or an explanation of Scripture; he told him to get up and eat. When we are feeling discouraged, we often turn away from ordinary activities. But most of the time, when God comes to us, he doesn't bring visions. He gives us the inspiration to do the simplest, most natural things—things we would never have imagined he was in. As we do them, we discover him there.

Discouragement is an inevitable part of human experience. It's in the nature of a rock to never be sad, not of a human being. If we were never sorrowful, we would never be overjoyed. We have a capacity for delight and sadness both, and it is only normal that we should be brought low by certain things.

In times of difficulty, our safeguard lies in doing what God asks of us, however small and insignificant his request may seem. If instead we try to block out our sadness, if we ignore it or push it down, we will only succeed in deepening it. But if we sense intuitively that the Spirit wants us to do something and we do it, our sadness begins to lift. Immediately we arise and obey; we enter a higher plane of life.

The Initiative against Despair

Rise! Let us go!

MATTHEW 26:46

In the garden of Gethsemane, Jesus's disciples fell asleep when they were supposed to be keeping watch. When they awoke and realized that Jesus was about to be taken, they were filled with despair.

We might imagine that this kind of despair is unusual; in fact, it's a very common human experience. Whenever we realize that we've done something we can't undo, whenever we let a magnificent opportunity pass us by, despair is the natural response. Sometimes, our feeling of despair is so deep we can't lift ourselves out of it. At these moments, we need Jesus Christ to come to us and say, "Rise! Let us go!"

When our Lord comes to us in this way, he tells us to accept the reality of our situation. "That opportunity is lost forever," he says. "You can't change what has happened. But rise now, and go on." In Gethsemane, the disciples had done something they felt was unforgivable. Jesus came with his spiritual initiative against despair, telling them to move on to the next thing. What is the next thing? If we are inspired by God, the next thing is always to trust him absolutely and to pray on the ground of his redemption.

Never let a sense of failure alter your new plans and actions. Let the past sleep, but let it sleep with Christ. Step out into the irresistible future with him.

The Initiative against Drudgery

Arise, shine, for your light has come, and the
glory of the LORD rises upon you.

ISAIAH 60:1

Drudgery—that hard, dull, seemingly unimportant work that no one wants to do—is one of the finest tests of character there is. Drudge work is utterly lowly and grubby. It requires us to get our hands dirty. It requires us to make an effort when we feel no motivation or divine inspiration. With drudgery, we have to take the first step as if there were no God. It's no use waiting for God to help us: he will not. But the second we arise, we find he is there.

Whenever we come into contact with drudgery, we know immediately whether or not we are spiritually real. In the book of John, we see Jesus—God incarnate, the highest and holiest of beings—doing the lowliest kind of work: washing feet. "No servant is greater than his master," he tells the disciples (13:16). Jesus brings himself down to the level of a servant, yet the moment he begins performing his lowly task, the work is transfigured. God's light shines upon it, and it stops being lowly and becomes divine. Whenever we allow God to do a thing through us, he always transfigures it into something divine, just as he took on human flesh and transfigured it.

Every person who has the Holy Spirit dwelling inside them is a divine temple for our Lord. Keep this in mind whenever you're faced with drudgery. If you arise and shine, no matter the task, the glory of the Lord will rise with you.

The Initiative against Daydreaming

Come now; let us leave.

JOHN 14:31

Dreaming and planning in order to do a task well is a good thing; daydreaming when we should already be doing is wrong. In John 14, Jesus gives a wonderful message to his disciples: "Very truly I tell you, whoever believes in me will do the works I have been doing, and they will do even greater things than these" (v. 12). We might expect that, after delivering this message, Jesus would tell the disciples to go off and meditate on what he'd said. Instead, he tells them to spring into action: "Come now; let us leave."

There are moments when dreaming is appropriate. If we are patiently waiting before God and he says, "Come with me by yourselves to a quiet place," this is an invitation to sit with him in contemplation (Mark 6:31). It's God's way of getting us alone so he can tell us what he wants us to do. But after he's told us, we have to watch out if, instead of taking action, we're inclined to keep dreaming about what he's said. God's blessing is never on idleness. When we get his wake-up call, we must go out and obey, leaving our dreams safely where we found them—with God, the source of all our dreams and joys and delights.

Taking action is the way we show Jesus we love him. When you're in love, do you spend all your time sitting around, daydreaming about your beloved? No! You get up and do something about it. That is what Jesus Christ expects.

Have You Ever Been Carried Away for Him?

"Leave her alone," said Jesus. "Why are you bothering her? She has done a beautiful thing to me."

MARK 14:6

If love does not carry us beyond ourselves, it is not love. If love is always discreet, always wise, always sensible and calculating, it is not love. It may be affection or warmth of feeling, but it does not have the true nature of love in it.

In Mark 14, Mary of Bethany is so carried away by her love for Jesus that she breaks a bottle of precious perfume and pours the fragrance over his head. Have I ever done something like this for God, not because it is my duty or there is some reward in it for me but just because I love him? If you are spending all your time marveling about the magnificence of the redemption, remember that there are valuable things you could be doing for the Redeemer. Not colossal, divine things: simple, human things that show God you genuinely love him.

There are times when it seems as though God is watching just to see if we will abandon ourselves to him. It's as though he wants to catch us in a natural, spontaneous, affectionate action. Abandonment is of more value to God than personal holiness. Personal holiness fixes the eye on its own spotlessness. When we fixate on our own holiness, we obsess over how we walk and talk and look. We become fearful of offending God, anxiously wondering if we're useful. If we come to the conclusion that no, we aren't, we are near the truth. It is never a question of being useful but of being of value to God himself. When we are abandoned to God, he works through us all the time.

The Discipline of Spiritual Tenacity

Be still, and know that I am God.

PSALM 46:10

Tenacity is more than endurance; it's endurance combined with the absolute certainty that what we expect to happen is going to happen. Tenacity isn't simply hanging on. Hanging on can be a weakness, a sign that we're too afraid to let go. Tenacity is the supreme effort of refusing to believe that our hero is going to be defeated. As disciples, our greatest fear isn't that we will be damned. It's that Jesus Christ will be defeated, and that the things he stood for—love and justice and forgiveness and kindness—won't win out in the end. God calls us to the discipline of spiritual tenacity. He asks us to do more than simply hang on. He asks us to work deliberately for him in the certainty that he's not going to be defeated.

If we are disappointed and losing hope just now, it means that we are being purified. There is nothing noble the human mind has ever hoped for or dreamed of that will not be fulfilled. One of the greatest stresses in life is the stress of waiting for God. But God has promised that our patience will be rewarded. "Since you have kept my command to endure patiently, I will also keep you from the hour of trial" (Revelation 3:10).

Remain spiritually tenacious.

The Determination to Serve

The Son of Man did not come to be served, but to serve.

MATTHEW 20:28

Paul's idea of service is the same as our Lord's. Jesus said, "I am among you as one who serves" (Luke 22:27). Paul echoed him: "For what we preach is not ourselves, but Jesus Christ as Lord, and ourselves as your servants for Jesus' sake" (2 Corinthians 4:5).

We have the idea that Jesus's ministers are called to be different kinds of beings, that they should be higher and holier than other people. Jesus said his ministers should be other people's doormats: spiritual leaders, not superiors. When Paul wrote, "We commend ourselves in every way: in great endurance; in troubles, hardships and distresses," he was describing the lengths he would go to as Christ's servant (6:4). He wanted to spend himself to the last penny; he didn't care if people stepped all over him.

Paul didn't draw his motivation for serving from a love for humanity. The well he drew from was his love for Jesus Christ. If we are devoted to the cause of humanity, we will soon be crushed and brokenhearted—we may often meet with more ingratitude from humanity than we might from a dog! But if our motive is to love God, no amount of ingratitude will keep us from serving.

Paul's experience of how Jesus Christ had dealt with him is the secret of his determination to serve others: "Even though I was once a blasphemer and a persecutor and a violent man, I was shown mercy" (1 Timothy 1:13). Paul realized that others could never treat him as badly as he'd treated Jesus. When we too come to this realization—when we see that Jesus Christ has served us despite our selfishness and cruelty and sin—nothing we meet with from others can shake our determination to serve them in his name.

The Delight of Sacrifice

I will very gladly spend for you everything I have.

2 CORINTHIANS 12:15

When the Spirit of God has filled our hearts with the love of God, we begin to identify ourselves with Jesus's interest in other people—and Jesus is interested in everyone. As his disciples, we have no right to be guided by personal preferences or prejudices. The delight of sacrifice comes from laying down our lives—not from carelessly flinging our lives away or giving them over to a cause but from deliberately laying them down for Jesus and his interests in others.

Paul laid down his life in order to win people to Jesus, not to himself. He sought to attract people to Jesus, never to himself (1 Corinthians 1:13). "I have become," he wrote, "all things to all people so that by all possible means I might save some" (9:22). To do this, Paul had to become a living sacrament. He didn't hide away or insist on a holy life alone with God, a life in which he'd be no use to others. Instead, Paul told Jesus to help himself to his life.

Many of us are so caught up in pursuing our own goals that Jesus can't help himself to our lives. Paul didn't have any goals of his own. "I could wish that I myself were cursed and cut off from Christ for the sake of my people," he wrote (Romans 9:3). Wild, extravagant talk, isn't it? No. When a person is in love, it isn't extravagant to talk like this, and Paul was in love with Jesus Christ.

The Poverty of Service

If I love you more, will you love me less?

2 CORINTHIANS 12:15

Natural love expects to be returned, but Paul didn't care if he was loved by those he served. He was willing to be ridiculed and overlooked, to be made poor and humble, just so long as he was bringing people to God. "For you know the grace of our Lord Jesus Christ, that though he was rich, yet for your sake he became poor" (2 Corinthians 8:9). Giving his all wasn't a burden for Paul; it was a joy: "I will very gladly spend for you everything I have and expend myself as well" (12:15).

The way Jesus thinks about service is not the way the world thinks about it. Jesus Christ out-socialists socialists. He says that in his kingdom the greatest will be the servant of all (Matthew 23:11). The real test for us lies not in preaching the gospel but in washing feet, in doing the things that are little esteemed by the world but count for everything with God.

Paul didn't care what God's interests in other people cost him. The instant God asks us to serve, we start making calculations. "God wants me to go there?" we say. "What about the salary? What about the weather? A sensible person has to consider these things." When we think like this, we're being selfish and cautious about how we serve God.

Paul was never cautious. He embodied Jesus's idea of a New Testament disciple, one who not only proclaimed the gospel but became, for the sake of others, broken bread and poured-out wine in the hands of Jesus Christ.

Doubts about Jesus

"Sir," the woman said, "you have nothing to draw with and
the well is deep. Where can you get this living water?"

JOHN 4:11

When Jesus told the Samaritan woman that he could give her living
water, her reply was full of doubt. We marvel at this story, because
we know our Lord has told the woman the truth. But when it comes to
our own lives, we aren't always so sure. "I'm impressed with the wondrous
things he says," we think. "But in reality, they can't be done!"

Where do our doubts about Jesus come from? They might spring from
other people's doubts about the plans we've made with God—their questions about where we'll get our money or how we'll live. Or we might
plant the seeds of doubt ourselves, informing Jesus that our problems are
too much, even for him.

What's really happening is that we've confused Jesus's limitations with
our own. We look at our own abilities to determine what Jesus can do,
then panic when we see the depths of our own inadequacy. "No, no,"
we protest. "I have no doubts about Jesus, only about myself." This is a
pious kind of fraud. None of us are truly confused about ourselves: we
know perfectly well what we can and can't do. But we do have doubts
about Jesus. Sometimes we even act insulted by his power, as though
we're hurt by the idea that he can do what we can't.

If you sense doubts about Jesus in yourself, bring them to the light
and confess them: "Lord, I've had doubts about you. I haven't believed
in your strength apart from my own. I haven't believed in your almighty
power apart from my finite understanding of it." Then ask God to take
your doubts away.

The Almighty God

"Sir," the woman said, "you have nothing to
draw with and the well is deep."

JOHN 4:11

The well is deep—indeed! The well of human nature is even deeper
than the Samaritan woman knew. Think of the depths inside you, the
depths of your thoughts and your feelings, of your hopes and your fears.
Do you believe that no depth is too deep for Jesus?

Imagine that there is a fathomless well of trouble inside your heart. Then
Jesus comes and says, "Do not let your hearts be troubled" (John 14:1).
Do you reply, "But, Lord, the well is too deep. You'll never draw quietness
and comfort up from it"? It's true; he won't. Jesus doesn't bring anything
up from the wells of human nature. He brings it down from God above.

If we're looking inside ourselves for the answers, diving into the wells
of our incompleteness, we'll only succeed in placing limits on God. Sometimes, we limit God by forgetting what he's done for us; sometimes, we
limit him by remembering. We remember how far we've allowed him to go
for us in the past, and we think that he can never go any further. But God
has no limits; God is almighty. As disciples, we must believe this fully. To
believe in God's almightiness means believing in the very thing that seems
to challenge it. We find it easy to believe that God can sympathize with us,
but when it comes to something we've already decided is impossible, we
shrug and say, "God can't do everything." God's ministry is infinitely rich;
we impoverish it when we talk like this.

The reason some of us are such poor specimens of discipleship is that
we don't believe in an almighty God. We have Christian attributes and
experiences, but we aren't abandoned to our Lord. Beware of the satisfac
tion that comes from sinking back and saying, "It can't be done." You
know it can, if you look to Jesus.

Do You Now Believe?

Now we can see that you know all things. . . . This makes us believe.

JOHN 16:30

When the disciples finally told Jesus that they believed he was the Son of God, Jesus replied with skepticism: "Do you now believe? . . . You will leave me all alone" (John 16:31–32). Many Christians leave Jesus alone as they go about their work. They're motivated by their conscience or a sense of duty, but their souls aren't in intimate contact with their Lord; they're leaning on their own understanding. It isn't a sin to work for God in this way, and there's no punishment attached to it, but when we catch ourselves acting like this, when we realize we've grown distant from Jesus and produced confusion and sadness for ourselves, we come back to him with shame and contrition.

We need to learn to rely on the resurrection life of Jesus on a much deeper level, to get into the habit of steadily referring everything back to him. We make decisions based on common sense, then ask God to bless those decisions. He cannot. Common sense is not in God's domain; it is severed from divine reality. Common sense tells us that duty and moral obligation should be our guides. "I *must* do this; conscience compels me," we say, haughtily. A decision based on common sense can always be backed up by an argument like this. But when we do something purely out of obedience to the Lord, no commonsense argument is possible. That's why obedience is so easy to ridicule.

If we don't want to leave Jesus alone, we must be willing to be ridiculed for his sake. We aren't told to walk in the light of conscience or of duty; we're told to walk in the light as God is in the light (1 John 1:7).

What Do You Want the Lord to Do for You?

Lord, I want to see.

LUKE 18:41

What is the thing that not only disturbs you but makes you a disturbance? It is always something you cannot deal with yourself. The solution is to get into direct contact with the Lord, and turn your problem over to him.

The man in Luke 18:41 has a problem he can't solve: he is blind, and he wishes to see. He knows he needs Jesus, and he shouts for help. "[They] rebuked him and told him to be quiet, but he shouted all the more" (Luke 18:39). The man shouts until he is allowed to come face-to-face with the Lord.

This is what we too must do, whenever we have a problem we can't solve. People will offer commonsense solutions, but God doesn't work in commonsense ways; he works in supernatural ways. Don't deify common sense, and don't limit God with memories of what you've allowed him to do in the past. "I've always failed at this and I always will," you say. "It's ridiculous to keep asking God to do it." If a thing seems impossible, it is the *exact thing* you need to ask for. God does the absolutely impossible.

What is your impossible thing? Is it to become so identified with the Lord that there's nothing of your old life left? God will accomplish this for you, if you ask. But you have to come to the place where you believe him to be almighty. When we look to God himself, we discover that doing the impossible comes naturally to him. Then—finally—we will ask for what we want. We've been in agony, trapped in the ignorance of our own hearts, all because we refused to ask.

The Piercing Question

Jesus said to Simon Peter, "Simon son of John, do you love me?"

JOHN 21:15

No sin can pierce us as deeply as the question Jesus asks of Simon Peter: "Do you love me?" Sin dulls feelings; the word of God intensifies them. When Jesus asks if we love him, the feelings brought up by his question are so intense they hurt. *Do* we love him? Or are we fooling ourselves?

It is impossible to be casual when Jesus asks this question. Peter's early love for Jesus was temperamental, professed in the whim of a moment and a mood. He loved Jesus on a purely natural level, in the way any person loves another who is good. It took the hurt of Jesus's question for Peter to realize that true love never merely professes anything: it pierces straight to the core of our personality, directing not only our words but everything we do.

Unless we get hurt right out of deceiving ourselves, the word of God isn't having its way with us. His word is sharp: "sharper than any double-edged sword, it penetrates even to dividing soul and spirit, joints and marrow" (Hebrews 4:12). Jesus's question strikes against all our illusions, reaching past our selfish individuality into the very center of our being—a terribly painful thing. But to be hurt like this by Jesus is the most exquisite hurt imaginable. It stings away every delusion and doubt, every selfish thought and worry.

When the Lord sends the hurt of his word to his child, there is no mistaking it. But the point of the hurt is the great point of revelation: it reveals to us how we truly feel about our Lord. "Lord," said Peter, "you know that I love you" (John 21:17).

Have You Felt
the Hurt of the Lord?

Peter was hurt because Jesus asked him the third time, "Do you
love me?" He said, "Lord, . . . you know that I love you."

JOHN 21:17

Have you ever felt the hurt of the Lord in the very center of your
being—the place where your real sensitivity lies? The devil never
hurts us there. Sin never hurts us there. Human emotion never hurts us
there. Nothing gets through to this place but the word of God.

A third time Jesus asked if Peter loved him. Peter was hurt because he
was waking up to an amazing fact: he *did* love Jesus, all the way through to
the core of his being. Peter had begun to see what Jesus's patient, repeated
questioning meant. It meant that Peter no longer belonged to himself. It
meant that, for Peter, there was no one in heaven above or on earth below
except Jesus Christ. It meant that Peter could never delude himself again.
It was a revelation to Peter to realize how much he truly did love the Lord,
and with amazement he said, "You know that I love you."

How skillful, patient, and direct was Jesus Christ with Peter! Our
Lord's questions always reveal us to ourselves, but he never asks until
the right time. Peter did not know how much he loved Jesus until the
patient, painful questions came. Probably once in each of our lives, the
Lord backs us into a corner and hurts us with this probing question,
until we realize that we do love him, far more deeply than any mere
declaration can tell.

The Unrelieved Quest

Jesus said, "Feed my sheep."

JOHN 21:17

This is love in the making: Peter, having confessed how deeply he loves Jesus, is told to add action to emotion and feed God's sheep.

The love of God was not created; love is God's very nature. When we receive the Holy Spirit, we are united with God so that his love is manifested in us. But this isn't the end of the story. The ultimate goal is that we may be one with the Father as Jesus is. "Holy Father, protect them by the power of your name, the name you gave me, so that they may be one as we are one" (John 17:11). What kind of oneness is this? Such a oneness that the Father's purpose for the Son becomes the Son's purpose for us: "As the Father has sent me, I am sending you" (20:21).

After Peter recognized the depth of his love for Jesus, Jesus made his point: Spend it. Don't declare how much you love me. Don't testify about the marvelous revelation you've had. "Feed my sheep." This is a challenging request, because Jesus has some extraordinarily funny sheep! Bedraggled, dirty sheep; awkward, headbutting sheep; sheep that have gone astray (Luke 15:3–7). God's love pays no attention to such quirks and differences. If I love my Lord, I have no business being guided by personal preference. I simply have to feed his sheep. There is no relief and no release from this part of the call.

Beware of letting your natural human sympathy decide which sheep you'll feed. You are called to spend *God's* love, not pass off a counterfeit version of it. That would end in blaspheming the love of God.

Could This Be True of Me?

I consider my life worth nothing to me.

ACTS 20:24

It's easier to serve God without a calling than with one. It's easier to be unbothered by his requirements and to let common sense be your guide—common sense with a thin veneer of Christian sentiment on top. If you choose to serve God in this way, you'll be more successful and leisure-hearted. But if you have received the call, the memory of it will never let you be. Once you receive a commission from Jesus Christ, it is impossible to continue working for the Lord on the basis of common sense.

What do you truly value? If you haven't been gripped by Jesus, you value your own acts of service, your own offerings to God, your own life. You take on practical work in his name, not because you've been called to it but because you want to be appreciated by the people around you. "Look how useful I am," you think. "Look how valuable." Practical work often competes with abandoning yourself to God. Instead of letting Jesus Christ tell you where to go and what to do, you follow your own commonsense judgment about where you'll be most valued.

The Holy Spirit warned Paul that "prison and hardships" awaited him, should he choose to follow Jesus Christ (Acts 20:23). Acts 20:24 reveals Paul's almost sublime annoyance at the idea that he would consider himself. His own life, he says, is worth nothing to him. The only thing that matters to him is fulfilling the ministry he's been given, and he refuses to use his energy for anything else. He is absolutely indifferent to anything except completing the Lord's task.

Never consider whether you are useful. *Ever* consider that you belong not to yourself but to him.

Is He Really Lord?

So that I might finish my course with joy, and the
ministry, which I have received of the Lord Jesus.

ACTS 20:24 KJV

Joy comes from the ultimate fulfillment of my life's purpose—that for which I was created and reborn. It doesn't come from the successful performance of a task. Jesus's joy lay in doing what the Father had sent him to do, and this is also where our joy lies: "As the Father has sent me, I am sending you" (John 20:21).

Have I received a ministry from the Lord? If so, I have to be loyal to it. I have to count my life precious only for its fulfillment. Think of the joy and satisfaction that will come from hearing Jesus say, "Well done, good and faithful servant!" (Matthew 25:21). We all have to find our place in life, and spiritually we find it when we receive our ministry from the Lord. First, though, we must get to know Jesus as more than our personal savior; we must know him as an intimate companion. Only then will he reveal to us our purpose.

"Do you love me?" Jesus asked Peter. "Feed my sheep" (John 21:17). Notice how Jesus doesn't offer Peter, doesn't offer *us*, a choice about how to serve. The only possibility is absolute loyalty to his command, absolute loyalty to what we discern when we are close to him.

Sometimes we misunderstand the call. We think that we are being called by a certain need—the need of God's children to hear the gospel, for instance, or to have someone intervene for them in prayer. But the need isn't what's calling us; the need is simply an *opportunity* for answering the call. The call itself is a call to absolute loyalty. God wants you to be loyal to the ministry you receive when you are close to him, whatever it may be. This doesn't imply that there is a specific campaign of service marked out for you, but it does mean that you will have to ignore the demands for service along other lines.

Amid a Crowd
of Paltry Things

As servants of God we commend ourselves in every way: in
great endurance; in troubles, hardships and distresses.

2 CORINTHIANS 6:4

It takes almighty grace to take the next step—the next step in devotion, the next step in our studies, the next step in the kitchen, the next step in our duty—when there's nothing to inspire us and no one to cheer us on. When there's no vision from God and no enthusiasm, when it's just the daily routine and the trivial task, it takes almighty grace.

Sometimes, it requires far more of the grace of God to take the next step than it does to preach the gospel. Perhaps at one time we had a clear vision of something God wanted us to accomplish, and we threw ourselves into it with excitement. But now the excitement has waned and we wonder how we'll keep going. We begin to doubt that the vision will ever be realized. It will be, if we'll keep working steadily until it is fulfilled. Every Christian has to participate in the essence of the incarnation; we have to bring it down into flesh-and-blood life and work it out through our fingertips. In the long run, what counts for God—and for people—is steady, persevering work in the unseen (2 Corinthians 4:18). The only way to live our lives uncrushed is to live looking to God.

Ask God to keep the eyes of your spirit open to the risen Christ, and it will be impossible for drudgery to crush you. Continually get away from pettiness of mind and thought. Remember Jesus's example: "Now that I, your Lord and Teacher, have washed your feet, you also should wash one another's feet" (John 13:14).

67

Undaunted Radiance

In all these things we are more than conquerors
through him who loved us.

ROMANS 8:37

In all these things. Paul is speaking here of things that might seem likely to separate the sanctified soul from the love of God. But the remarkable thing is that nothing can separate the two. Certain things can and do come between God and our devotional practices or private life with him. But nothing can separate the sanctified soul from his love.

The bedrock of Christian faith is the unearned, fathomless marvel of the love of God displayed on the cross, a love we never can and never will deserve. Paul says that this is the reason we are "more than conquerors through him who loved us." We are *super*-victors through Christ, and the joy we take in this fact is directly related to the magnitude of the challenges we face.

The wave that distresses the new swimmer gives the seasoned surfer the extreme joy of riding clean through it. For the sanctified soul, tribulation, distress, and persecution are not things to fight or fear or avoid: they are sources of jubilation. In them, we are more than conquerors through Christ—not in spite of them but in the middle of them. If certain things didn't seem likely to overwhelm us, we wouldn't fully appreciate Christ's victory. We know the joy of the Lord not in spite of hardship but because of it. "In all our troubles my joy knows no bounds," Paul says (2 Corinthians 7:4).

Undaunted radiance is not built on anything passing. It is built on the love of God, which nothing can alter. The experiences of life, however terrible or monotonous, are powerless to touch it.

The Relinquished Life

I have been crucified with Christ and I no
longer live, but Christ lives in me.

GALATIANS 2:20

It is impossible to be united with Christ unless we are willing to let go: to let go not only of sin but of our entire way of looking at things. In 1 Timothy 6:19, Paul writes that God wants us to "take hold of the life that is truly life." But before we can take hold, we must let go. If we wish to be born from above in the Spirit, the first thing we have to let go of is pretending we're something we're not. What our Lord wants us to present to him isn't goodness or honesty or endeavor; it's real, solid sin. In exchange, he gives us real, solid righteousness. First, though, we must give up the idea that we are worthy of God's consideration; we must give up the thought that we are anything at all. After we do, the Spirit will show us what *else* there is to relinquish. The giving up must happen repeatedly, in every phase. Every step of the way, we must give up the claim to our right to ourselves.

Am I willing to relinquish my hold on my possessions and affections? On everything? Am I willing to be identified with the death of Jesus? There is always a painful shattering of illusions before we finally do relinquish.

When we truly see ourselves as the Lord sees us, it isn't the abominable sins of the flesh that shock us; it's the awful nature of pride in our hearts against Jesus Christ. When we see ourselves in the light of the Lord, shame and horror and desperate conviction strike home. If you have come to the point where you must relinquish or turn back, go on through. Relinquish all, and God will make you fit for what he requires.

Going with Jesus

"You do not want to leave too, do you?" Jesus asked the Twelve.

JOHN 6:67

Our Lord's words hit home most forcefully when he talks in simple ways. Like the disciples in this passage, we are aware of who Jesus is; we know him and love him. But he still asks if we are going to leave him. Why? Jesus wants to drive home that the attitude we have to maintain toward him is one of total trust and abandon. We must always be journeying forth in his name, following wherever he leads. "From this time many of his disciples turned back and no longer followed him" (John 6:66). These disciples lost the bold and reckless commitment Jesus wanted them to have. They didn't stop believing or fall back into sin, but they gave up their intimacy with him.

Many of us today are guilty of this. We may be spending ourselves and being spent in Jesus's name, but we aren't walking with him; we aren't drawing close to him with perfect trust and confidence. Yet this is the one thing God holds us to steadily: that we be one with Jesus as Jesus is one with the Father.

After Christ is formed inside us, the discipline of our spiritual life centers on this question of oneness. If God gives you a clear and emphatic message about something he wants you to accomplish, let oneness be your guide in how to pursue it. Don't struggle to find any particular method; don't create a plan that isn't his. Simply live a natural life of absolute dependence on Jesus Christ, and God will bring about the thing he wants.

Never try to live in any way other than God's, and remember that God's way is absolute devotion to him. The certainty that I know I do not know—that is the secret of going with Jesus.

Have a Message and Be One

Preach the word.

2 TIMOTHY 4:2

We aren't saved to be mere mouthpieces for God; we're saved to be his sons and daughters. God has no interest in turning his preachers into passive channels. He wants vigorous, alert, wide-awake men and women with all their powers and faculties intact. God's disciples are spiritual messengers, not spiritual mediums, and the message they deliver must be part of themselves.

The Son of God *was* his message. His words were Spirit and life (John 6:63). As disciples, we must become the examples of what we preach; our lives must become the very sacrament of our message. It is natural to want to serve and give to others—that desire lies in most human hearts. But it takes a heart broken by the conviction of sin, sanctified by the Holy Spirit, and crumpled into the purposes of God to turn a life into the sacrament of its message.

There is a difference between giving testimony and preaching. Anyone who is saved can give testimony. A preacher is someone who has answered the call of God and is determined to use every power to proclaim God's truth. God takes his preachers out of their own ideas for their lives and shapes them for his use, just as the disciples were after Pentecost. Pentecost did not teach the disciples anything; it *made* them the embodiment of their message: "You will be my witnesses" (Acts 1:8).

Before God's message can liberate other souls, the liberation must be real in you. Gather the material you wish to preach, and set it alight. Let God have perfect liberty when you speak.

Vision

I was not disobedient to the vision from heaven.

ACTS 26:19

When Jesus Christ appeared to Paul and told him to preach the gospel, there was nothing hesitant about Paul's response: he obeyed, keeping the vision from heaven bright before him as he began fulfilling his commission (Acts 26:12–19). If we lose the vision, we alone are responsible; it means that we've been lax and careless in our spiritual lives. The only way to be obedient to the vision God sends is to give our utmost for his highest, and this can only be done by continually and resolutely recalling the vision, while working steadily to realize it. The test is to keep the vision in our sights not only during times of prayer and devotion but sixty seconds of every minute, sixty minutes of every hour.

"Though it linger, wait for it" (Habakkuk 2:3). We cannot rush the fulfillment of a vision; we have to live in its light until it accomplishes itself through us. Sometimes, after we receive a vision, we grow impatient. We go racing off into practical work, hoping to speed things along. Then the work becomes our focus, and we lose sight of the vision. We don't even notice when it has been fulfilled! Working to realize the vision is necessary, but we must work *steadily*, without rush or force, and only when and where God chooses. Our ability to wait for the vision that lingers is a test of our loyalty to him.

After God gives a vision to his disciple, he always sends a whirlwind, flinging his disciple to the place where the seed of the vision will take root and grow. Are you ready to be sown, so that the vision can fulfill itself through you? The answer depends on whether or not you're living in the light of what you've seen. Let God fling you out, and don't go until he does. If you try to dictate where you'll go, you'll prove empty. But if you let God sow you, you will bring forth fruit.

Our Abandonment to Him

Then Peter spoke up, "We have left everything to follow you!"

MARK 10:28

Jesus replies to Peter that the disciples will be amply rewarded for their sacrifice. But he also makes clear that their reason for following him shouldn't be anything they'll get in return. It must be entirely for Jesus himself: "for me and the gospel" (Mark 10:29).

Beware of an abandonment that has a self-interested spirit in it. Too often, we abandon ourselves to God because we want to be made holy or delivered from sin. We will be, if we are rightly related to him, but this demanding spirit is not in line with the essential nature of Christianity.

Abandonment is not for any *thing* at all. We've become so commercialized in our thinking that we go to God only when we want something. It's as if we're saying, "I don't want you, God. I want myself: a clean, Spirit-filled version of myself. I want to be put on display in your showroom, and to be able to say, 'See what God has done for me.'"

If we give something to God only because we want something in return, there is nothing of the Holy Spirit in our abandonment: it is miserable, commercial self-interest. To gain heaven, to be delivered from sin, to be made useful to God: real abandonment never considers these things. Real abandonment is a personal sovereign preference for Jesus Christ himself.

When we are forced to choose between our natural relationships and Jesus Christ, most of us desert him. "I did hear your call, Lord," we say. "But my spouse needs me; my mother needs me; my self-interest needs me." "Such a person," Jesus replies, "cannot be my disciple" (Luke 14:26). It is always natural devotion that tests abandonment. Rise to the test, and God will embrace all those you hurt when you abandoned yourself to him.

His Abandonment to Us

For God so loved the world that he gave his one and only Son, that
whoever believes in him shall not perish but have eternal life.

JOHN 3:16

We will never understand how to abandon ourselves to God until
we understand how God abandoned himself to us. When God
gave his Son in love to the world, he didn't give just a part of himself. He
gave all of himself, absolutely and entirely. He gave with total abandon,
holding nothing back. We must beware of talking about abandonment if
we don't really know about it, and we won't know—not until we realize
the full meaning of John 3:16.

That God gave with total abandon is the very essence of salvation.
Salvation isn't merely deliverance from sin or the experience of personal
holiness. Salvation is deliverance out of self and into union with God.
What I *experience* of salvation may be a sense of personal holiness, but
what salvation actually means is that the Spirit of God has brought me
into contact with God himself. I am thrilled by the contact with something infinitely greater than myself, and I wonder how it is possible. It is
possible because God has given himself completely for our sake.

Abandonment is never self-conscious. If we are abandoned to God,
our whole life is his. There is no awareness of striving to let go, no struggling to abandon. We aren't torn between our old life and our new. We
are simply given over to our Lord. Our entire existence is wrapped up
in him, and the consequences of abandoning ourselves never enter into
our thinking.

Obedience

You are slaves of the one you obey.

ROMANS 6:16

The first thing to do when confronting a habit or mindset that controls me is to face an unwelcome fact: I am responsible for being controlled, because at some point I gave in. If I am a slave to myself—to my habits and urges, my egotisms and selfishness—I am to blame, because I gave in to myself. Likewise, if I obey God, it's because I've yielded myself to him.

We learn the truth of this in the most ridiculously small things. "I can give up that habit whenever I want," you say. You cannot. Try it, and you will find that the habit absolutely dominates you. Give in to selfishness in childhood, and you will find it the most binding tyranny on earth. Yield for one second to any form of lust—to the thought "I must have this thing at once"—and you will be chained to that thing, even if you hate yourself for it.

No human power can break the bondage of a character that has been shaped by giving in. Only the power of the redemption is sufficient. You must yield yourself in utter humiliation to the only one who can set you free, the Lord Jesus Christ: "He has sent me to proclaim freedom for the prisoners and . . . to set the oppressed free" (Luke 4:18). Only Jesus can break the chains of slavery to yourself, and only when you let him. Yield yourself to the Lord, and he will set you free.

The Discipline of Dismay

Those who followed were afraid.

MARK 10:32

When I first began walking with Jesus, I was sure I knew all about him. It was a delight to give everything up for his sake, to fling myself out on a risky path of love. Now, I'm not so sure. Jesus is striding ahead of me, and he looks strange: "They were on their way up to Jerusalem, with Jesus leading the way, and the disciples were astonished, while those who followed were afraid" (Mark 10:32).

There is a side to Jesus that chills the heart and makes the spiritual life gasp for breath. This strange being, with his face set like flint and his striding determination, no longer appears as counselor and comrade. He has a point of view I know nothing about. At first, I was confident that I understood him, but now there is a distance between us; I can no longer be so familiar with my Lord. He is out ahead, and he never turns around.

Jesus Christ had to fathom every sin and every sorrow that could possibly afflict the human race: this is what makes him seem so strange. When we see him in this aspect, we don't know him. He is a leader striding before us, and with dismay we realize that we don't know how to follow him. We have no idea where he's going, and the destination has become strangely far off. A sense of darkness surrounds us.

The discipline of dismay is a necessary part of discipleship. The danger is that we will try to escape the darkness by kindling a fire of our own. God says we must not: "Let the one who walks in the dark, who has no light, trust in the name of the LORD" (Isaiah 50:10). When the darkness of dismay comes, endure until it is over. Out of it will come a following of Jesus which is an unspeakable joy.

The Judgment Seat of Christ

For we must all appear before the judgment seat of Christ.

2 CORINTHIANS 5:10

Paul says that, no matter who we are, we must appear before the judgment seat of Christ. We tend to think of this moment of judgment as some far-off event, but it needn't be. Right here and now, we can learn to live in the white light of Christ's penetrating gaze. However difficult his judgment may be to face at first, it will eventually bring us delight, revealing all the wonderful work God has done inside us.

Keep yourself steadily before Christ's judgment, and remember his command: "Do not judge" (Matthew 7:1). A wrong temper of mind about another soul will end in the spirit of the devil, no matter how saintly you are. One worldly judgment about another person, and the end of it will be hell inside you.

Whenever you are tempted to judge, drag the impulse at once to the light and say, "My God, I am guilty." If you don't, hardness will set in. It isn't only God who punishes us for sin. Sin establishes itself in the sinner and pays the sinner back in full: the price is that, gradually, you become so used to sinning that you no longer recognize it as sin.

No amount of struggling or praying will enable us to stop sinning. It takes the power of the Holy Spirit to come in and set it right. "Walk in the light, as he is in the light" (1 John 1:7). Many of us think that walking in the light means walking according to the standard we've set for other people. That is not God's standard. Walk in the light of the holiest you know—the Lord Jesus Christ—and let his judgment have its way with you.

The Ruling Passion

We make it our goal to please him.

2 CORINTHIANS 5:9

Staying focused on the goal Paul sets in 2 Corinthians 5:9 is difficult work. It means holding ourselves, year in and year out, to the highest ideal: not the ideal of winning souls or establishing churches or ushering in revivals but the ideal of pleasing Jesus Christ. Failure in spiritual work isn't caused by a lack of spiritual experience; it's caused by a lack of effort to maintain the highest ideal.

At least once a week, take stock before God and see if you are keeping your life up to the standard he has set. The standard must be your ruling passion, your master ambition. Paul is like a musician who cares nothing about the approval of his audience—so long as he catches the look of approval from his master.

Follow a lesser ambition to its natural conclusion, and you will see why it is so necessary to live facing the Lord. Any ambition that is separated from the highest goal, even by the tiniest degree, may end in our disqualification. "Therefore," Paul says, "I do not fight like a boxer beating the air. No, I strike a blow to my body and make it my slave so that after I have preached to others, I myself will not be disqualified for the prize" (1 Corinthians 9:26–27). Paul was constantly watching himself, constantly keeping himself in line, lest he lose sight of the ideal.

I have to learn to relate everything to the master ambition, maintaining it at all times. My worth to God in public is what I am in private. Is my master ambition to please him and be acceptable to him, or is it something less, no matter how noble?

Perfecting Holiness

Since we have these promises, dear friends, let us purify
ourselves . . . perfecting holiness out of reverence for God.

2 CORINTHIANS 7:1

Have I recognized that God, through his promises, has a claim on me? We delight in God's promises to us and count on their fulfillment, and it is right that we should. But Paul reminds us that this is only the human side of the equation. The divine side is that God wishes us to become pure and holy out of reverence to him.

Have I understood that my body is the temple of the Holy Spirit? Or do I have a habit that obviously can't stand the light of God upon it? Through sanctification, the Son of God is formed inside me, but the story doesn't end there. I must transform my natural, physical life into a spiritual life through obedience. God educates us down to the scruple, examining every aspect of our character. Keep yourself clean in your daily walk, and when God begins his inspection, rid yourself at once of any impurity his gaze reveals. The goal is to bring yourself, in both body and spirit, into perfect harmony with the nature of God.

Are my thoughts and outlook in perfect agreement with the Spirit inside me? Or am I intellectually defiant? Am I forming the mind of Christ and obeying God? Jesus never spoke of his right to himself. Rather, he maintained an inner watchfulness, continually submitting his spirit to his Father. I too have the responsibility of keeping my spirit in agreement with the Lord's Spirit. If I do, then by degrees Jesus will lift me up to where he lived—in perfect consecration to his Father's will, paying no attention to anything else.

Am I perfecting this kind of holiness in the fear of God? Is God getting his way with me? Are other people seeing more and more evidence of him in my life? Be serious with God and happily leave the rest alone. Literally, put God first.

The Faith of Abraham

By faith Abraham . . . obeyed and went, even though
he did not know where he was going.

HEBREWS 11:8

In the Old Testament, people demonstrated a close, personal relationship with God by separating themselves physically from friends, family, and home. Abraham "obeyed and went," leaving everything behind. Today, the separation God asks of us is more of a mental and moral separation. We must maintain a radically different mindset from those who do not have a personal relationship with him, even if they happen to be our nearest and dearest. "If anyone comes to me and does not hate father and mother," Jesus said, "such a person cannot be my disciple" (Luke 14:26).

As disciples, we are called to walk by faith. Faith never knows where it is being led, but it knows and loves the One who is leading. It is a life of *faith*, not of intellect and reason. It is a life of knowing the One who sends us out. The root of faith is knowledge of a person—Jesus Christ himself. One of the biggest traps we fall into is the idea that God will surely lead us to worldly success. He will surely lead us into a personal relationship with Jesus. That is his measure of success.

The final stage of the life of faith is the development of our character. There are many moments in our walk with God when we feel our character being transformed. We might feel God's blessings wrap around us when we pray, and for a moment we are changed. Then we go back to the ordinary days and ways and the sense of glory vanishes. The life of faith isn't a life of mounting up with wings but a life of walking and not fainting (Isaiah 40:31). It isn't a question of sanctification but of something infinitely greater: of faith that has been tried and has stood the test. This was the faith of Abraham, a tried-and-tested faith built on a real God. "Abram believed the LORD" (Genesis 15:6).

Friendship with God

Then the LORD said, "Shall I hide from
Abraham what I am about to do?"

GENESIS 18:17

Chapter 18 of Genesis brings out the delights and difficulties of real friendship with God.

Its delights. Real friendship with God is different from occasionally sensing his presence in prayer. To have a real friendship with God is to be in such close contact with him that you never need to ask him to show you his will. It is to be nearing the final stage of the life of faith. When you are rightly related to God, life is full of liberty and delight: you *are* God's will. Unless he tells you otherwise, your commonsense decisions are his will for you, decided in perfect friendship with him.

Its difficulties. In Genesis 18, Abraham begins to plead with God to spare Sodom, but he stops before receiving God's final assurance (vv. 25–33). Why did Abraham stop praying when he did? He was not yet intimate enough with God to go boldly on until his desire was granted. There was something still lacking in their relationship. Whenever we stop short in prayer, there is another stage to go in friendship with God. We aren't as intimate with God as Jesus was and as God wishes us to be.

What was the last thing you prayed about? Were you devoted to your desire or to God? Did you hope to get some gift of the Spirit, or to get at God himself? "Your Father knows what you need before you ask him" (Matthew 6:8). The point of asking is to get to know God better. "Take delight in the LORD, and he will give you the desires of your heart" (Psalm 37:4). Keep praying in order to get a perfect understanding of God himself.

Interest or Identification?

I have been crucified with Christ.

GALATIANS 2:20

Paul doesn't say, "I've decided to imitate Christ" or "I'm interested in following Christ." He says, "I have been crucified with Christ": he has become identified with Christ in Christ's death.

In my spiritual life, the essential need is to sign the death warrant of my sinful disposition. I must issue a moral verdict against the idea that I have a right to myself, drawing on every emotional and intellectual tool at my disposal to make the decision Paul made. When I do, when I come to the decision to identify myself with Christ's death, everything that Christ won on the cross is realized in me. By freely committing myself to God, I allow the Holy Spirit to impart to me the holiness of Jesus Christ.

"The life I now live in the body, I live by faith in the Son of God" (Galatians 2:20). My individual life continues, but the wellspring of my character, my ruling disposition, is radically altered. My body remains as it was, but the satanic belief I used to have—the belief in my right to myself—is destroyed. Paul emphasizes that he is living this life "now." It isn't a life he *plans* to live one day; it's the life he's living "in the body"—the body that other people can see. This body bears witness to the life of Christ within it: "And I no longer live, but Christ lives in me" (v. 20).

The Burning Heart

Were not our hearts burning within us?

LUKE 24:32

We need to learn the secret of the burning heart. Jesus appears to us, the fires are kindled, and we have wonderful visions. Then normal life resumes, and the flame dies down. The burning heart is a heart that can go through anything, but first we must learn how to keep the flame alive. The dull, bald, dreary, commonplace day, with its commonplace duties and people, kills the burning heart—unless we learn the secret of abiding in Jesus.

If we are abiding in Jesus, keeping him at the forefront of our minds and letting him guide all our decisions, nothing we meet with will be able to kill the flame inside us. But if we lose sight of the Lord, the emotion he kindled when we were close to him will fade. It isn't just drudgery and duty that can make this happen; it's our unwillingness to let the emotion have its way.

Much of our distress as Christians is caused not by sin but by ignorance of our own natures. For instance, to know if we should allow a certain emotion to have its way with us, all we need to do is think about the outcome of the emotion. If we push the emotion to its logical conclusion and find that it's something God would condemn, we shouldn't follow it. But if it's an emotion kindled by the Spirit and we don't allow it to have its way, it will drop us to a lower level. The higher the emotion, the deeper the degradation if the emotion is not worked out in the way God wants.

When the Spirit kindles an emotion inside you and your heart begins to burn, let it burn. Do everything you can to help the emotion along. Don't build up barriers against it or make excuses about why you can't follow it, however inconvenient or illogical it may seem. Abide in Jesus, and keep the flame alive.

The Struggle with Worldliness

For since there is jealousy and quarreling among you, are
you not worldly? Are you not acting like mere humans?

1 CORINTHIANS 3:3

People who haven't been born again in the Spirit know nothing about
the struggle Paul describes in 1 Corinthians 3:3. The war between the
flesh and the Spirit begins with spiritual rebirth and can only be resolved
in one way: we must learn, Paul says to "walk by the Spirit"; if we do, we
"will not gratify the desires of the flesh" (Galatians 5:16), and our struggle
with worldliness will disappear.

Are you contentious and easily troubled? We imagine that no Christian ever is, but Paul says we are, and he connects these qualities with
worldliness. Is there a truth in the Bible that instantly irritates you? It's
proof that you're still worldly. If sanctification is being worked out in
you, if the Spirit of God is getting his way in your life, there is no trace
of the contentious spirit left.

Whenever the Spirit of God detects something wrong, he doesn't ask
you to make it right; he asks you to accept the light so *he* can make it right.
A child of the light confesses instantly and stands naked before God. A
child of darkness is defensive and says, "Oh, I can explain that away."
When the light breaks and you feel convicted of having done wrong, be a
child of the light. Confess, and God will deal with it. If you try to excuse
or vindicate yourself, you will prove yourself a child of darkness.

How will you know that your worldliness has gone? God will see that
you have any number of opportunities to prove to yourself the marvel of
his grace. He will send you practical tests, again and again, until you see
that you are changed: "If this had happened before," you'll say, "I would
have been filled with resentment!" When worldliness is gone, it is the
most obvious thing imaginable. You'll never cease to be amazed at what
God has done for you on the inside.

He Increases, I Decrease

He must become greater; I must become less.

JOHN 3:30

As a disciple of Jesus Christ, your great responsibility is to be a friend of the bridegroom, following the example set by John the Baptist: "The friend who attends the bridegroom waits and listens for him" (John 3:29). The bridegroom's friend never takes the central role away from Jesus or becomes a necessity to another person's soul. If you find, in your relationships with others, that you have stolen the spotlight away from Christ, then you know that you are out of God's established order for his disciples. You'll know your influence over others has taken the right direction when you see their souls gripped by the claims of Jesus Christ.

Never interfere when another person's soul has been gripped by Christ. However painful it may appear to you from the outside, pray that the pain grows ten times stronger, until there is no power on earth or in hell that can keep that soul away from the Lord. You may often see Jesus Christ wreck a life before he saves it. Never mind what havoc the bridegroom causes, what crumblings of health and wealth. Rejoice with divine hilarity when his voice is heard.

Over and over again, we turn ourselves into amateur providences, trying to prevent suffering by stopping God. In the end, our sympathy costs other people dearly. One day, they'll accuse us of being thieves, of stealing their affections away from their bridegroom and causing them to lose their vision of him. We must beware of rejoicing with a soul in the wrong thing, but we must make sure to rejoice in the right thing. The bridegroom's friend "is full of joy when he hears the bridegroom's voice. That joy is mine, and it is now complete. He must become greater; I must become less" (John 3:29–30). John the Baptist is describing the absolute effacement of the disciple; he will never be thought of again. But he acknowledges this with joy, not sadness.

The Most Delicate Mission on Earth

The friend who attends the bridegroom waits and listens for him.

JOHN 3:29

Goodness and purity should never attract attention to themselves; they should be magnets that draw attention to Jesus Christ. If my holiness isn't drawing people to him, it isn't holiness of the right order; it's an influence that will spark misplaced affection and lead souls astray. A talented and virtuous preacher may be an obstacle if, instead of preaching Jesus Christ, he preaches only what Jesus Christ has done for him. People will come away saying, "That preacher has a fine character!" when they should be coming away with Jesus himself. If my face is growing brighter while Jesus's fades, I'm not being a true friend of the bridegroom (John 3:30).

In order to maintain a loyal friendship with Jesus, we have to be careful with our moral and vital relationship to him—more careful than we are with anything else, even our obedience to God. Sometimes, the only thing we need to do is maintain this vital connection. Occasionally, when we are faced with a crisis, we have to seek knowledge of God's will so that we can act in obedience. But most of life doesn't require this kind of conscious obedience; it requires the maintenance of this relationship, our friendship with the bridegroom.

Beware of allowing anything to come between you and Jesus Christ. Too often, Christian work provides the perfect excuse for breaking our soul's concentration on him. Instead of being friends of the bridegroom, we may end up working against him.

Vision by Personal Purity

Blessed are the pure in heart, for they will see God.

MATTHEW 5:8

Purity is not innocence; it is much more. Purity is the outcome of sustained spiritual closeness with God. We have to grow in purity. Our private life with God may be healthy, and our inner purity may be unsullied, and still, every now and again, the bloom on the outside may become tarnished.

God doesn't shield us from this possibility. When we go astray in some outward expression or action, we realize just how necessary outward purity is to maintaining our vision of God. Spiritual understanding becomes blurred the instant we go astray in our external lives. When we notice that the outward bloom of our life with God has been damaged, even to a tiny degree, we must stop everything and correct it. The inner sanctuary and the outer rooms must be brought into perfect agreement.

God makes us pure by his sovereign grace, but we also have something we must take care of: our bodily lives. Our bodily lives bring us into contact with other people and other points of view, and if we are not careful these external influences can tarnish our purity. If we are going to keep in personal contact with Jesus, there are some things we must refuse to do or touch or think, even things which seem worthy and legitimate to others. A practical way of maintaining personal purity around other people is to say to yourself, "That man, that woman: perfect in Christ Jesus! That friend, that relative: perfect in Christ Jesus!"

Remember that spiritual vision depends on character: "Blessed are the pure in heart, for they will see God."

Vision by Personal Character

Come up here, and I will show you.

REVELATION 4:1

Elevated emotions can only come out of an elevated habit of personal character. If you've developed the kind of character that allows you to live up to the highest standards you know, God will grant you insights that draw you even higher. He will continually say to you, "Come up here, and I will show you."

Each time you go higher, you will face new and different kinds of temptation. The golden rule of temptation is "go higher." Both God and Satan use the promise of elevation to draw us upward, but they use it to very different effects. Satan whispers to us of an unattainable holiness, a holiness beyond what flesh and blood can bear. He draws us into a spiritual acrobatic performance that ends up freezing us: we are poised on a tightrope and cannot move. But when God, by his grace, elevates us to the heavenly places, we find a vast plateau, where we can move around with liberty and ease.

Compare this week in your spiritual history with the same week last year, and see how God has called you higher. This is how you know you have grown in grace—not because you no longer backslide into sin but because God has granted you new spiritual insight. If God has revealed to you a new truth, you know it is because of growth in your character. Keep trusting and obeying him. Whenever he gives you a truth, apply it instantly to your life. Always work it out in your personal practices; always keep yourself in its light.

"Shall I hide from Abraham what I am about to do?" (Genesis 18:17). Why didn't God immediately tell Abraham about his plan to destroy Sodom and Gomorrah? Because Abraham wasn't yet ready to receive that truth. God has to hide from us what he does, until by personal character we get to the place where he can reveal it.

There Must Be Some Misunderstanding

"But Rabbi," they said, "a short while ago the Jews there
tried to stone you, and yet you are going back?"

JOHN 11:8

At times, we are like the disciples in John 11: confused about what Jesus is saying and convinced that there must be some misunderstanding. It is dangerous to believe that simply because I don't understand Jesus, he must be mistaken. Perhaps I think that if I obey God's word, I'll bring dishonor to him. I won't. The only thing that brings dishonor to God is disobedience. To put my idea of his honor above what he is clearly telling me to do is never right, even if it's coming from a genuine desire to prevent his being slandered or shamed.

You can always tell when an instruction comes from God, because it comes with quiet persistence. When you begin to weigh the pros and cons, you bring in an element that isn't of God. This is when you risk coming to the conclusion that what he's saying must be a mistake.

Many of us are loyal to our own ideas about Jesus, but how many of us are loyal to *him*? Loyalty to Jesus means you step out even when there is no path; loyalty to your own ideas means that you try to map out the path first, using your own intelligence. Faith is not intelligent understanding; faith is deliberate commitment to a person when we see no way.

Are you loyal to Jesus, or to your idea of Jesus? Are you loyal to what he says, or are you trying to compromise, bringing in your own rationalizations? When he says something and you start to debate, it's because you have an idea of his honor that isn't right.

"Do whatever he tells you" (John 2:5). Stop debating, and obey your Lord with a glad and reckless joy.

Our Lord's Surprise Visits

You also must be ready, because the Son of Man will
come at an hour when you do not expect him.

LUKE 12:40

As disciples, we must be ready for Jesus to appear at every moment. This isn't easy, no matter what our experience is. Our battle isn't so much against sin or difficulties or circumstances; it's against being so absorbed in our work that we fail to notice the Son of Man when he comes. And yet, this is the great need: not answering questions about our beliefs or our creeds or whether we are useful but being ready for him.

Jesus rarely comes where we expect him. He comes where we do not expect him, and through the most illogical chains of events. The only way a disciple can be true to God is by being ready for the Lord's surprise visits. It isn't service that matters; it's intense spiritual reality; it's being ready to welcome Jesus Christ at every turn. This will give our life the attitude of childlike wonder God wants it to have. If we are going to be ready for Jesus, we have to stop being "religious." That is, we have to stop treating religion as a higher kind of culture and become spiritually real. When we are spiritually real, Jesus is able to use us as he likes; at any second, he can visit others through us.

If you are looking to Jesus, if you're setting your heart on what he wants and avoiding the call of the religious age you live in, you will be considered unpractical and dreamy. But when he appears in the burden and the heat of the day, you will be the one who is ready.

Trust no one who blocks your sight of Jesus Christ, not even the most devout Christian who ever walked the earth. Be always ready to greet the Lord, especially where you least expect him.

Holiness versus Hardness

I urge, then, first of all, that petitions, prayers, intercession
and thanksgiving be made for all people.

1 TIMOTHY 2:1

The reason many of us stop praying and become hard toward God is that our interest in prayer is merely sentimental. We read books that say prayer is beneficial, that it quiets the mind and uplifts the soul, and this makes us feel good. It makes us feel right to say we pray. But prayer, in God's eyes, must go together with intercession. One is impossible without the other.

To intercede in prayer on another's behalf is to seek the mind of God about that person. Too often, instead of worshipping during prayer, we construct arguments about how prayer works. "I don't see how you're going to do this," we say to God. If we're arguing with God like this, it's a sure sign that we aren't worshipping. We're hurling demands at his throne and dictating what we want him to do. When we lose sight of God, we become hard and dogmatic toward him. And when we become hard toward God, we become hard toward other people.

Are we worshipping when we pray, lifting our minds up to know God's thoughts? Are we living in a holy relationship to him? Or are we hard and dogmatic?

"He was appalled that there was no one to intervene" (Isaiah 59:16). If there is no one, do the job yourself. Become the one who worships God and lives in holy relationship to him. Commit to the hard work of intervening in prayer on others' behalf, and remember that it is, truly, *work*. But it is work that will sustain you, as the Lord's "own righteousness sustained him" (v. 16).